Praise for *The Bord*

"*The Borderland Between Worl..* a Pakistani-American woman trying to live in two w..... not quite belonging to either. Ayesha F. Hamid's deep desire to belong is complicated by schoolmates who bullied her as well as her parents' fear for her safety in a new country. Ayesha's journey is filled with obstacles and contradictions. This is an important story, especially in these times, for better understanding the struggle that is the immigrant experience."

— **Tori Bond**, author of *Familyism*

"Ayesha F. Hamid beautifully captures the dual-faceted story of a Pakistani immigrant trying to belong in the United States as well as the classic coming-of-age story in her debut memoir, *The Borderland Between Worlds*. Though her family could have lived comfortably in the upper class of their home country, they set out to build a new life in America. After a few difficult years, Ayesha sets out to live her dreams, facing fears and a variety of challenges along the way. I found myself, as a first-generation American and woman, cheering her on through every chapter and empathizing with her struggle of always having to decide between South Asian and American ways."

— **Elaine Paliatsas-Haughey**, founder of the Scars and Tattoos Project

"This memoir shows the classic struggle that all children of immigrants face when assimilating to American culture. Ayesha deals with opposition, from all sides, when she tries to assert her identity. *The Borderland Between Worlds* is an essential read for anyone wanting to learn more about the South Asian immigrant experience."

— **Lena Van**, event director at Philadelphia Stories

The Borderland Between Worlds

A Memoir

Ayesha F. Hamid

www.auctuspublishers.com

Copyright © 2020 Ayesha F. Hamid
Book and cover design by Sarah Eldridge

Published by Auctus Publishers
606 Merion Avenue, First Floor
Havertown, PA 19083
Printed in the United States of America

The Borderland Between Worlds is a work of creative non-fiction. The events recounted are to the best of the author's memory. Some names have been altered to protect the privacy of those involved.

All rights reserved. Scanning, uploading, and distribution of this book via the internet or via any other means without permission in writing from its publisher, Auctus Publishers, is illegal and punishable by law. Please purchase only authorized electronic edition.

ISBN 978-1-7334456-1-0 (electronic)
ISBN 978-1-7334456-0-3 (print)

Library of Congress Control Number: 2019952113

Foreword

All life forms must move to survive. We all move, and we are all immigrants. Countries and borders were created, not only to organize but also to control and divide. *The Borderland Between Worlds* is the long-expected, debut memoir of Ayesha F. Hamid, in which she uses her unique voice to show us the vicissitudes of an immigrant's life in the United States. Using the borderland as an allegory for the threshold of identity, Hamid presents a beautifully written memoir that gives us a space for dialogue. For her, borders are more than lines to cross and countries are more than physical spaces. We carry our places with us.

Growing up as a Pakistani woman in the United States, Ayesha had to deal with the constant struggles and challenges that a life in movement brings. But what is life, if not movement?

Ayesha takes us through the entire spectrum of human experience: from the deepest questioning about identity, belonging, and transcendence, to the vivid details of a private and interesting life, from her struggles with bullying in school to a tragic marriage, from race, religion, family, and self-discovery.

As a skilled author, Ms.Hamid doesn't hesitate in sharing details with her reader. Like a traveler opening her luggage after a long trip, she puts order to all the little things that she collected along the way, objects that show the reader the best and worst of the trip. This is how our talented author opens her heart to us, by sharing her life experiences from her home, the place where she really belongs: her unique writing.

Come, dear reader, to this trip where the question is not only "Who Am I?" as an existential quest derived from a vast diversity of deeply lived situations, but also "Who Are We?" The answers open the possibility to inclusivity and building a better world for those who will come after us.

Carlos José Pérez Sámano, contributing author of
Who Will Speak for America?

Preface

This is my story, but I hope that it will speak for others who have dealt with the pressures of not being able to fit into a world that oftentimes demands total conformity. This book is for those who understand the immigrant experience first-hand or who have had to simultaneously meet the demands of different worlds — worlds which can have diametrically opposed values, and worlds which are willing to punish when demands aren't met. It is for immigrants struggling to find a new home and a better life. It is for anyone who is teased for not meeting an ideal and for those who actually fit in but are kind enough to help those who don't. It is for the children who sit alone and embarrassed during lunch time and for those who continue to be bullied, terrorized even, for being different.

In this borderland, not fully belonging anywhere or with anyone is a great burden to bear – it feels like a space of cowering weakness, but it can be the place of incomparable strength. We walk between worlds, and in order to survive, we have had to make peace with everything and everyone. We are the only ones who can clearly see both sides and understand both worlds. We are *immigrants* who have found the way, and we are *the other*. We are the bridge that can end conflict. We bring peace.

The Borderland Between Worlds is a memoir containing my struggle and heartache, no greater or less than the heartache of many others like me. To the reader, some of the battles fought in this book might seem less trying than the struggles explored by other memoirists, struggles that may revolve around drug addiction or childhood abuse. Like other readers, I admire the strength of those who survive addiction or abuse and have the courage to write about their experiences. Nevertheless, simple events can also shape lives and determine direction.

Recreating my journey has been truly cathartic, and in writing this book, partly done to exorcise the proverbial ghosts of the past, I've stayed as true to my story as memory has allowed. Nevertheless, no matter how hard writers try, our memories are indeed selective, and even though I've tried to point out my own hypocrisy in dealing with different situations, I'm sure I've fallen short in capturing the entirety of actual events in an oftentimes chaotic life. The names of people involved, other identifying information, and the location of certain events have been changed to protect the anonymity of others and to lessen unnecessary distraction from the story. And in terms of the importance of names and words, when the word America is used in this book, it is used colloquially to refer to the United States of America. I have recently been reminded that, in actuality, the word America encompasses an entire continent that includes Central and South America.

I thank you for embarking on the journey and taking the time to read *The Borderland Between Worlds*. I hope your reading of this book contributes to the greater good, especially in the trying times in which we find ourselves when immigrants and other minorities are again being demonized, all over the world, for monetary and political gain. I also hope that this book will find its way into the hands of those who really need to hear the story of an ordinary person surviving the everyday challenges of isolation and hardship. For those of you who need it, I hope you are helped by the words that follow.

Ayesha F. Hamid

Chapter 1

Dreams

Everything was possible as I stepped off the cement porch and into the summer morning with heat spreading onto my tanned, brown skin. Having just turned twenty, the pervasive feeling of possibility expanded with the sun rising in its azure sky, but hope was tempered by an inconvenient fact. I needed to come up with thousands more, or else I couldn't return for my sophomore year at Chestnut Hill College, the private college I wanted to attend more than I wanted anything else in the world.

The three months before my sophomore year would be a test. The pursuit of fun was now meaningless, and frivolity, in all its forms, outlawed. I needed to find a way back – education was the only door open to someone like me. Being a Pakistani immigrant living in white suburbia, I already knew what it was like to be left out. College was the only place I ever fully belonged, so I wouldn't let it end up on the list of things I couldn't be a part of.

Finding a job was necessary, so I strode towards Montgomeryville Mall to find one, but would anyone hire me? As I reached the main road, the grey and bubbly concrete grain of the sidewalk scratched the surface of my sneakers. Stopping, I looked back at my parent's house, sitting at the bottom of Pioneer Circle, and took in the view of the neighborhood. The homes here had been built in the early nineties. Each house was a different color than its neighbor – moss, blue, or light yellow – the color of my parents' home. Despite the different colors, there was still a sense that every home was identical to its neighbor, built the same way and for the same reasons.

My family's yard sat right in the middle of the cul-de-sac. *Ammi* stood in the yard, looking towards me with her straight nose and dark, perfectly almond-shaped eyes. Her face and body were smaller than mine, and her black hair, tied back in a single braid, made for a stark contrast with her white, cotton *shalwar-kameez*.

Having always been interested in things that were traditionally feminine, like fabric, makeup, and jewelry, my mother's taste in fashion was refined. After coming to America though, she had neither the opportunity to dress in the same glamorous way she used to nor did she feel it necessary to do so. Though she didn't dress up anymore, she made sure to wear the basics – gold bangles, earrings, and a necklace. She waved to me and as she did, her bangles shook.

In terms of style, my mother and I were opposites. I was a tomboy, didn't accessorize, and wore clothing for its comfort rather than its appearance. Wearing loose khakis with a white dress shirt, I adjusted my glasses, covering big, brown eyes. My wavy, black hair bobbed back and forth below my waist. Having recently lost some weight, I was down to a hundred and forty. With my tall frame at nearly five-nine, this weight made me appear thin.

As I walked out of the door earlier, my mother stopped me to warn me. Looking up at my face, she reminded me to be aware of my surroundings.

"People are not always what they appear to be. Talk less to strangers, and you have less of a chance of running into a criminal," she said.

"I'll be fine," I said.

"You're a girl. Why are you walking the whole way to the mall by yourself?" she asked.

Her open-ended question was the perfect opportunity for adolescent sarcasm.

"*Because* that's what I have to do. I *wanted* a license and a car, and *that didn't happen*, so now I have to walk," I said.

"What you're wearing, your pants and shirt, it's too revealing. Whenever you wear pants instead of *shalwar-kameez*, I can always see the shape of your hips and rear-end. Your outfit will draw male attention, and it's already dangerous for you to be walking," she insisted.

"I'm not going to talk to strangers driving past me like I'm some idiot, and this outfit is a size larger than my actual size. It is beyond modest. *Ghuda hafiz*," I said.

"*Ghuda hafiz*," she said.

I was a smart, twenty-year old woman. Twenty for God's sakes. What was my mother freaking out about? She was overly concerned with my trip into town, unless I ran into a serial killer on the way, but who can really plan ahead for that? Besides, I didn't have time to think about things like crime and safety. Money remained in the forefront of my mind. At the start of summer vacation, time was still on my side, yet I didn't want this fact to blind me. The heat and haze would simmer for a time and then fade, dying out like a forcefully stricken match, expanding into explosion and then disappearing into nothing. The thought of summer break ending made me trek towards town more quickly.

As cars whizzed by, I became lost in thought and considered everything that had led me to that moment, and a familiar anger started to well up in me again. Why did I have to be one of the only people who didn't have a car or a license? *In this too, I had to be different.* My parents didn't want me driving because they thought me wild whereas everybody else, including my peers and teachers, saw me as a bookworm, only interested in things like grades, books, and college.

Being an adolescent was stressful enough, but the South Asian, Muslim, and female combination created crisis, and having to please the expectations of two cultures proved crushing. I desperately wanted to fit in, though I often didn't, and my parents inadvertently helped me to stick out. They forbade me from participating in anything besides academics for fear that too much involvement with the culture-at large jeopardize my safety and usurp my old-world values. And what was considered to be suspect by my parents – going on trips, to the movies, parties, or playing sports. So, even though I always yearned to be on a sports' team, I couldn't. Playing sports required girls to run around in shorts and tank tops, and what could be worse than that – for many Pakistani parents, only a handful of things, including drinking alcohol, gallivanting with boys, and sleeping over other people's houses.

In accordance with these views, my parents discouraged their children from spending time on diversions like dances, parties, sleepovers, and especially the dangerous business of dating, and by the time I turned seventeen, I started to agree that blocking out distractions was for the best.

Any passion I had, I funneled into my studies. Inadvertently, schooling became a world in which I experienced excitement as real as any other. The myriad restrictions that often ruled my psyche stopped holding sway in academia.

Regardless of everything that I couldn't be a part of, I felt entitled to my education. Not only did I feel in control of my studies, but I excelled at them. I'd gone from having bad grades in middle and grade school to having above average grades in high school where I'd been given a number of awards for academic achievement.

But it was never my parent's intention that I become obsessed with school, and they tried to curb my "all or nothing" attitude. The summer before college was supposed to start, they wanted me to consider taking a year off to achieve some balance.

"Take some time off from school and help with the business at home?" *Ammi* said.

"Why would I do that? I've been working towards college for a long time," I said.

"I just don't think there's a rush," she said.

"Of course there's a rush. I've been accepted to Penn State Abington and Chestnut Hill College. Chestnut Hill College gave me a scholarship, which will take care of most of my tuition. Why would I reject that offer and sit around not doing anything?"

In Pakistan, it was considered to be sinful to disagree with your parents, but I couldn't help arguing with them.

Fearful of all the contradictory influences surrounding me, my parents decided that they didn't want to take any chances with me, their only daughter – they thought my graduation from high school might be the right time for me to have an arranged marriage.

"We can take this time to go to Pakistan and find you a nice husband. You can continue your studies after you're married, and then, your husband can make sure you're safe," *Ammi* said.

"No way. You want me to throw all my work down the drain, but I'm not leaving school or marrying. How come no one else in this family has to be married off besides me? What about the boys? They're older. Why don't you marry them off first?"

My father overheard the conversation and added, "Why don't you sort some things out before you go to college? You don't even know what you want to do, and you can't even drive," he said.

"That's why I need to live on campus."

My parents exchanged a concerned look.

"I don't think that's a good idea either," *Ammi* said.

My mother didn't think I was mature enough to live on my own without attracting trouble and hated the thought of me living in a dorm where she wouldn't be able keep track of me and make sure I was safe. She'd heard about the dangers of dorm living from relatives who explained that living at college was the doorway to every possible vice. All manner of criminal activity could be found on American campuses, including drug abuse, prostitution, rape and murder.

"You trust people too much. Someone could kill you out there. Do you think we want to hear that our only daughter is missing or found in a field somewhere?" *Ammi* asked.

"It's so unfair. You treat me like this because I'm a girl."

"You just don't understand the world yet," was the typical response.

My father was more concerned that I'd fall into the snares of pre-marital sex, which was the epitome of failure for a good Pakistani girl.

Emphasizing the point over and over, he'd say things like, "this 'boyfriend shoyfriend' thing is unacceptable where we come from, and it is unacceptable in this house. A man is either a husband, or he's nothing. A husband is a *shareef* man who will take care of you and make sure you're okay. A boyfriend will use you for a time and dump you when he is done or worse."

It was like my father was running his very own boot camp for good Pakistani boys and girls and, on a daily basis, he'd drill us with the question, "what do good Pakistani children do?" and the appropriate responses from my brothers and I had to be things like, "stay at home with your parents," "don't go to parties," "never drink alcohol," and at all cost, "stay away from the opposite gender."

Neither my father nor my mother understood that they really didn't need to worry about parties, alcohol, or boys – I was too scared of getting into trouble to try alcohol or drugs, and was rarely, if ever, invited to a party. Boys were more interested in mocking me than dating me, and the message from most boys, whether I asked for their opinion or not, was that I didn't measure up. Sometimes those messages were sent in subtle ways, and other times, they were sent in not-so-subtle ways. Like one afternoon in high school, when my best friend Christy and I headed out of the cafeteria, a student that neither of us knew walked up to me and offered me his unsolicited opinion about my looks,

"You know something?" Looking down at me severely from sharp and unforgiving eyes, he said, "You are *ugly*. You really are. I watched you earlier when you were eating. I thought *phew* she is *ugly*. Fucking *loser*." He shook his head and walked away while others looked on.

As shocked as me, Christy gasped as her blue-green eyes teared up. She pushed back her long blond hair and stepped forward to hug me. No words were spoken, but her kindness, following those harsh words, caused me to sob. After a few moments, she spoke so that I didn't have to.

"Do you want to talk to the guidance counselor?" she asked. I nodded, and she took my elbow.

"Let's go," Christy said.

We walked out of the cafeteria together, and she went with me to the counselor's office. On the way towards the office, our conversation continued.

"Why did he say that?" I asked.

"He is an asshole, and what he said isn't true," she said.

"Are you sure? It seemed like he meant it." I said.

"He's a jerk. He doesn't know his ass from his elbow. Don't be sad about this. You aren't ugly, you're beautiful," she said.

I gave Christy a weak smile, but then, tears started to stream again. I relaxed my face, so I wouldn't start crying again.

As a young woman, my self-esteem wasn't steady enough for the degree of ridicule that I had to face, oftentimes on a daily basis. Where my family came from, humility was indoctrinated into children, not self-esteem; this had the positive effect of minimizing the ego but also having that ego crushed time and again. How could humility survive in a place that valued the ability to counterattack decisively when attacked? How could I avoid the bullying that plagued my life because I was not confident enough or rich enough or sexy enough or American enough or just "not enough" for the standards set by others?

No matter what though, I had Christy. I was so thankful for her; without kind people like her, I might have given up on the idea of a better future, but regardless of deliberate and regular blows directed at me, for reasons I didn't understand, with the help of people like Christy, I still managed to dream.

Chapter 2
Money Matters
❋ ❋ ❋ ❋ ❋

After an hour of dwelling on the past while walking towards Montgomeryville, I arrived at the main entrance of the mall. Entering through the double doors, I inhaled the encapsulating fragrance, a mixture of soap, candles, and cake mixed together – the aroma, penetrating, clean, and sweet, all in one. The floors and the store windows were polished to a shine. I took a deep breath and admired the glowing lights reflecting from the surrounding surfaces. The combination of light and sweet scent overwhelmed me. Becoming momentarily distracted, I wanted to walk and window-shop instead of looking for a job. Refocusing, I remembered my mission – I needed to prove myself to the world.

Heading towards the center of the mall, I scanned storefronts in the search of information. I stopped in front of a store called Science Exploration where large, clear windows were tucked into carved, wood paneling, in both the floor and ceiling of the store. An advertisement, taped onto one of the windows, read "Help Wanted."

Stepping in, I asked for an application, and after filling it out, was given an immediate interview with one of the assistant managers, Rebecca, a woman in her early twenties. Her curly, red hair and freckles made me think of Anne Shirley, the fictional, lovable little girl from Lucy Maud Montgomery's Book, *Anne of Green Gables*.

"So, it says you're going to Chestnut Hill College," she said.

"Yes, I really love it there. Are you going to college?" I asked.

"No, my husband and I both work full time and are saving up to start a family," she said.

She smiled at the mention of her husband. Though she was happily married, I felt sorry for the fact that, for whatever reason, Rebecca couldn't go to college.

"So, what would you say are your best qualities?" Rebecca asked as she wrote on a clipboard, which held my application.

"I'm dedicated, hard-working, and responsible," I said.

"What's a quality that you need to improve on?" she asked.

Discussions with family and friends flashed before my eyes. "Oh…that's a good question. Let me think. I would like to be less sensitive," I said.

"Well, that's something we can all work on," Rebecca said. The interview continued another five minutes. Open minded, Rebecca disregarded the fact that I didn't have any experience in retail and gave me the job. My excitement was obvious, so Rebecca smiled, sharing in my happiness.

I asked Rebecca if I could call my mother. Rebecca let me use the phone in the stockroom, though it was reserved for business calls. I told my mother that I'd been hired for a job in the mall, and that I needed to stay in the store to start my orientation.

"How late will you be out?" *Ammi* asked.

"Till eight, probably. Can you ask *Abba* to pick me up?" I said.

"That's too late. Are you going to do this all summer?" my mother asked.

"*I have to*," I said.

She hung up before I could say anything else.

I returned to the main floor and joined Rebecca behind the register. She described my job in detail while stacking counters with what looked like crystal. Handing me some additional paperwork to fill out, she continued on with her project.

Later, Rebecca explained that Science Exploration specialized in items related to intellectual exploration and inquiry, including educational material on astronomy, biology, botany, as well as other branches of science. Along with items geared towards scientific inquiry, the store also sold some less serious items like slinkys, water snakes, Chinese finger-traps, and yo-yos all stuffed into a large, translucent-plastic container, which was split up into smaller compartments for each item. So, Slinkys had their own bin, yo-yos their own, and so on. The most exquisite items in the store were the fine, collectible, crystal formations, ranging in color from Amethyst and Indigo to Aquamarine.

Rebecca said that I'd work as a part-time sales assistant and my priority would be to help the customers with questions and to man the cash registers. When there was a lull in customers, I'd work on organizing, stacking, and refilling sold-out items.

So at my first job, the tasks I focused on paled in comparison to the exciting things I'd been involved with during my first year at Chestnut Hill College where I had a voice and contributed to an ongoing intellectual conversation with professors and peers about the state of the world and how to improve it. At Science Exploration, I had to focus on the needs of my employer and nothing else, but during breaks that summer, I spent time reading in B. Dalton Bookstore and dreamed about going back to school and continuing with my classes.

Following hours of familiarizing myself with the store's products, my first workday ended. Realizing it would take a while for *Abba* to arrive, I stood near the front entrance of the mall, again admiring the reflection of light bouncing off every clean surface. After an hour's wait, his car finally pulled up. Standing all day had made my feet hurt horribly, and it was nice to sit down on the cool leather seats of his Lincoln Town Car.

"*Ammi* said you have a job? How do you like it?" he asked.

"It's good. My boss is nice, and hopefully I'll be able to make enough for next year's tuition," I said.

Suddenly, his cell phone buzzed; it was a call from one of his employees. My parents, after being in the United States for just two decades, would soon be the owners of a thriving town car service, from which a considerable revenue would be earned, but their success would come too late to help me with my educational expenses.

As he answered his call, my father's expressive, green eyes widened. His thick, curly hair was cut short, and regardless of the fact that he'd put on some weight, my father was still a good-looking man with kind eyes and a warm smile. He stayed on the phone for the rest of the ride home.

Chapter 3
Boundaries
❋ ❋ ❋ ❋ ❋

When we arrived back at Pioneer Circle, I noticed that the neighbors were still out, sitting in their yards. Something about their lawns bothered me – perhaps their sense of uniformity, or the fact that you couldn't really tell one lawn from the other. In fact, all the yards were nearly perfect. Pioneer Circle was full of gardening enthusiasts, driven by the pursuit of flawless yards, and every bright green and weed free lawn was expertly cut, complete with lines where the mower clipped the grass.

My family, on the other hand, rarely tended to the lawn. One reason for our lack of conformity was my mother's strong, albeit unorthodox views about avoiding the use of chemicals as much as possible. Her views made us all opposed to using anything "unnatural" on the lawn, including pesticides and fertilizers.

My parents may also have been blasé about gardening because no one expected them to do yard work where they came from. Those living in Karachi's suburbs, like my parents, had servants to take care of manual labor like gardening, cleaning, and cooking. In Pakistan, servants were in plenty because no middle class existed. You were either rich or poor, and if you were poor, you served the rich.

But in Lansdale, an American suburb, the fact that our family remained so casual about our lawn, drove our neighbors crazy, especially those living on either side of us. After we moved into the neighborhood, the biggest dilemma for our neighbors to the right, the Smiths, was to find a way of avoiding the eyesore that was our lawn. To solve this problem, they erected huge evergreens between their property and ours. Not wanting to convince us of right and wrong, the Smiths believed us to be damned in the realm of property values.

The Russos, on the other hand, especially Mr. Russo, didn't believe us beyond redemption. He wanted to make us understand that a well-kept lawn could elevate your home's property value, as well as the value of the entire neighborhood. Angry at our state of affairs, he couldn't believe that the Habib family had moved to Pioneer Circle without knowing any of the rules. During our first few of years in the neighborhood, Mr. Russo paced back and forth, enraged at our ineptitude. Once in a while, he'd blow up.

"What is wrong with you people, why don't you take care of your lawn? What planet do you come from?" Mr. Russo shouted.

Why did he put us down so much? Did he hate us because of our lawn or because we were from a "different planet" as he mocked? Over the years, my family found out the real reasons for his anger. As part of a middle class, struggling to maintain its lives and means, Mr. Russo and his wife worked various odd jobs to make ends meet. The family's daily grind exhausted them and, at times, made them irritable and erratic. Taking all this into consideration, it wasn't a surprise that property values were so important to them.

My father and Mr. Russo started to exchange stories about their lives. Relating to Mr. Russo, my father took a genuine interest in listening to him. After some time, something amazing happened – Mr. Russo and my father became friends. It turned out that the Russos weren't motivated by racism although, over the years, I'd run into my fair share of actual bigotry.

Our family came to understand our neighbors – what was first seen as obsession with gardening came to be understood as something unavoidable. My opinion of the neighbors, who at first seemed to be closed-minded, changed when I saw them facing some of the same trials that my parents went through. Their pain, whether hidden or apparent, made them more similar to us than anything else, and yes, we were not so different from each other after all.

Still, for my family, a feeling of isolation persisted, and, for me, my neighborhood wasn't the only place where that feeling was perceptible. Throughout my time in school, I was left out by classmates and, sometimes, even some of my teachers. Boundaries formed from the fact that I wasn't really "one of them," and I could see eyes rolling when I spoke as if I actually belonged. I knew it was the same for my brothers because they didn't have any friends and usually brought home bad grades.

In school, other children were also excluded for stupid and arbitrary reasons like where they lived, who their parents were, and what they liked to do. The "popular kids" were all identical while the "ordinary kids" were full of variation. Ordinary kids outnumbered popular ones because being popular meant fitting into a specific mold that many could not. As with many other things in life, money, or lack thereof, seemed to determine your popularity. If your parents had money, you lived in certain places, had certain tastes, and enjoyed particular activities. You had a right to call yourself the best, be the best, and laugh at others who didn't meet your standards.

What else did it mean to be popular? It meant your parents had excellent connections, connections who could help you out of a variety of trouble, motivate you to reach for unimaginable goals, help you enter the right colleges, and even persuade others to give you scholarships. You were gifted with a new car when you turned sixteen and were remarkably attractive due to your brimming confidence, in addition to your flawless physique. Your wardrobe was filled with brand names, and you were usually of European descent.

Had my family not ventured away from Pakistan, my life would also have been the life of an insider and one of ease. So, if the choice had been mine, would I have given up everything I'd learned from coming to a new country, and what is learned by every immigrant who comes here, that breadth of wisdom and sadness pushing us down with its weight, leaving dents in our bones, our skulls, and our souls? Would I have opted for security over the truth of what life can be? Would I have taken the easy way out?

No, I don't think so. If the decision had been mine, then I too would have brought my family to this land. I'd have yelled out, "It's not a mistake. America is not a mistake! It's the way our lives are meant to unfold. And if we stay in Pakistan, where everything is easier, then we will miss out on the struggle and the learning. Most importantly, we will miss out on each other – in America, sometimes, all we will have is each other, and we'll have to work together to try to make sense of it all."

And, no I wouldn't do anything differently than how life actually unfolded. Staying in Pakistan would surely have meant an easier life, but I would have lost the undeniable truth I've learned about my life and the lives of others, which is that human existence is tenuous, temporary, and chaotic, and there is no certainty.

Yet, one part of me grieved, with my parents, at everything we'd lost in our transition to a new nation. Another part of me welcomed our challenges. Growing up, I wasn't going to let the fact that my parents struggled financially and that my classmates referred to me as "the Indian girl," stop me. I aspired towards respectable heights, whether others believed I could reach them or not, and although I was different, I luckily never lacked supporters. Many of my teachers wanted me to thrive and gave me endless support; their encouragement was sacrosanct.

Mr. Likens was one of the teachers who helped in maintaining my hopes; interacting with him made me feel smart and optimistic about my future, and his manners, intelligence, and congeniality made him somebody I looked up to. It was the ultimate compliment that he found merit in my thoughts. During a class focusing on powers of government Mr. Likens asked,

"What phrase describes the idea that the three branches of the federal government interact to maintain equilibrium?"

Excited that I knew the answer, I raised my hand and said, "The phrase is *the balance of power.*"

"Very good, Ayesha. Could you also please describe the functions of the three branches of government?"

Having memorized the answer the night before, I answered the question correctly and in detail. Mr. Likens smiled, and as he did, appreciation filled my heart because if he admired my intelligence, then maybe one day, I could be as smart and as accomplished as him.

Chapter 4
Exclusion and Escape

✹ ✹ ✹ ✹ ✹

I readied myself for my second day of work at Montgomeryville Mall. As I left the house, my mother looked at me disapprovingly. A young woman walking into town, alone, seemed very unusual to her. At my age, she never went anywhere without a chaperone, but Karachi in the early seventies, when my mother was twenty, couldn't be compared to Lansdale, Pennsylvania.

Since my dad wasn't there to give me a ride, I left the house an hour before I needed to arrive at work. Walking towards the mall, I reeled as cars sped by, screeching and pulling me towards the road with their gravity. My walk gave me time to consider everything further, and one thought kept bothering me – why didn't I have a license like everyone else my age? In my last year of high school, a majority of the senior class drove to school. Everyone else had fun, shared rides, and met up for breakfast before school started. What did they talk about at those breakfasts? I'd have done anything to listen to their conversations.

I watched student drivers from my seat in the school bus, and they reminded me of celebrities stepping out from new cars with cute clothing, sun glasses, and movie star hair. My classmates' ability to drive spoke of freedom. Like so many other activities, driving was something I longed to do but could only observe from afar.

In terms of my goal of becoming a licensed driver, everything and everyone worked against me. Though they didn't forbid me from pursuing my license, I could feel my parent's silent disapproval – they viewed my teenage rebellion and me having a driver's license to be a disastrous combination. So, they never encouraged my hopes of having my own car. The family car, a Lincoln Town Car, was the size of a small boat and not helpful for driving practice, and parallel parking was a trick of the devil meant to keep decent people, like me, from passing their driver's license tests. I'd already failed the parallel parking portion of my driver's test a couple of times.

As I contemplated these challenges, one thought suddenly quieted every other – *you'll fail this time, like you always fail. There's no point in trying.* This type of pessimistic logic sometimes superseded everything else, as if a network of neurons performed their calculations and deduced that I'd already unsuccessfully attempted the driver's license test a few times. To my brain, defeat was a statistical fact with a hundred percent probability. The bigger question was whether failure would be limited to my driver's license test or whether everything else in my life would follow suit? Considering this, my body, as it habitually did, isolated my hopes. It sent me the sure signal that it wanted no more of it, the endless cycle of dreams and disappointment, not just about the license but about everything, including education, belonging, and love. It demanded that I give up my longing for faith. It desired the solitude and quiet that could be found in a space where there weren't any winners or losers, any success or failure. My body wanted an escape from itself; quite simply, it longed for an end.

When I arrived at work, I was overwhelmed by my thoughts but glad to see Rebecca. I spent the day training with her though feelings of embarrassment and failure remained in mind. Throughout the shift though, Rebecca's reassuring nature helped me to stay on task.

As soon as I returned home after work, I ran up the stairs to my room and put on music, becoming absorbed in the sound as the singer's voice came through the headphones. Sarah Mc-Lachlan's voice, with its Mezzo-Soprano range, possessed the capabilities of an array of musical instruments combined. At times, she sang like a violin with melancholy cries, and at other times, she became a flute or harp leading the listener to a juxtaposition of emotion – joy and lamentation experienced simultaneously with her exhalations. As I lay there, listening to her CD, *Stumbling towards Ecstasy*, with the windows open to let in the air, her song soothed me. Quieted like a drowsy child listening to a lullaby, I collapsed into sleep.

Waking up the next morning, I told my mother I needed to go to work again. She asked, "Are you going to have to work every day?"

"I have to work if I want to save up enough money to pay for school," I said.

"Maybe you should go to a state school instead of Chestnut Hill College," she said.

"How can I go to a state school? State schools have *boys*. You would all make me miserable, if I was going to a school with *boys*. Remember high school? Why do you think I'm going to a girl's school in the first place? State school equals boys. Chestnut Hill equals no boys. It's not a hard decision. I'm leaving," I said.

"Shut up and go then, *badthameez*," my mother said.

Both *Ammi* and *Abba* looked critically at the fact that so many American high school and college students were bogged down with the rigor of a job and unable to focus fully on their studies. Growing up as members of the Pakistani upper class, my parents didn't relate to studying and working at the same time, and neither of them had a job before they completed their degrees. When my parents lived in Pakistan, families in the upper class had many luxuries, whereas the poor lacked basic necessities. So, as members of the upper class, my parents focused on their future while their counterparts lived drastically different lives; the poor in Pakistan lived a life of uncertainty and toil, the same difficulties that now marked my existence.

Regardless of their high standard of living in Pakistan though, my family ventured away from its homeland – in their early thirties, my parents just picked everything up and opted to start over in a completely new country and culture.

I'd have done the same if the decision had been mine because, in Pakistan, all we had heard was that America was a sort of salvation – a place where people lived freely and never wanted for anything, a place as close to paradise as possible and, most importantly, a heaven free from disease.

Karachi, on the other hand, was a hotbed of communicable disease, like all other tropical cities. While there, my family saw its fair share of sickness – my mother experienced two, life-threatening illnesses by the time she reached thirty. Nearly losing her life as a child, she contracted a vehement strain of typhoid. My grandparents watched on as their eldest child struggled for her life. Stuck in fever and paralysis for weeks, my mother won her fight. She'd survived, but it wasn't going to be the last time that the city's grim reaper, a particularly calculating sentinel, visited her home.

After her wedding, my mother had three children, one baby right after the other. I was the third child and a lucky one at that. While pregnant with me, my mother fought another life threatening disease.

"It might be lung cancer" her doctor told her "since all the treatments for tuberculosis have been unresponsive." With a weakened body and a confused mind, my mother gave birth to me in June of 1978. Her weight dropped below a hundred pounds. Those around her whispered that she looked more like a skeleton than a woman. As she saw the stares, she couldn't help but listen. Forced to consider finality, the convincing quick sands of fear dragged her deeper into an abyss. Maybe it was true. Maybe 1978 would be her last year on earth. The tuberculosis had already taken its toll and would eventually take her life.

My mother told my father that her time might be limited.

"I'm so weak. I feel like there's nothing left of me," she said.

"You need to be brave. You can't give up like you're already done for," he said, holding her shoulders for encouragement.

"Why did this have to happen to me? I'm so worried about the children. What's going to happen to the children?" she asked, leaning her head on her hands.

"You need to think about fighting your own illness first, and then you can start thinking about the kids. They're being taken care of, and you are not," he said.

"I don't trust other people to take care of them. What if someone's watching them and forgets? What if they're dropped?" my mother asked.

"They will be okay. You have to go overseas for treatment," my father said.

"I don't want to go anywhere. Nasir just had croup. I can't leave the kids!" she said, struggling.

"The treatment here isn't working. You have to try something else," he said.

"If something happens to me, please stay with the kids," she pleaded.

An optimist by nature, my father couldn't accept the fact that his young wife had come to terms with the possibility of her death.

"No one's going to let anything happen to you," he said.

After this conversation, everyone around my mother hurled themselves into action and, inadvertently, my family's exploration of the West began.

Regardless of familial consensus though, my mother wouldn't change her mind about going abroad for medical treatment. She told her father why she couldn't leave.

"I can't abandon the children. They're so little. What if something happens? It's not right," my mother said.

"You're in no state to take care of anyone else. Why don't you understand that you have to take care of yourself?" he asked her.

"But, it feels like I'm deserting them," she said.

"It may feel like that, but if you stay here, you will have to leave them forever," he said.

This proved to be the pivotal conversation that changed her mind, and then, she agreed to go abroad. She made the journey to England with the help of her sister, Aliya. After arriving in England, intensive treatment of my mother's tuberculosis began, and her new doctors provided the kind of treatment she hadn't yet received. Feeling the breath of life, her beaten body started a slow recovery, and within a few months, she actually put on weight, pounds she desperately needed. By the end of her stay in England, she'd fully recovered, and her recovery convinced my family that the West had come closer to solving the mysteries surrounding death and disease.

Yet, my family wasn't yet free from unforeseen illness – health problems confronted my family again when my little brother, Irfan, arrived. Much to the dismay of my parents, he suffered from severe digestive problems at birth. At pivotal points in his early life, he couldn't keep down any nourishment.

Irfan's doctor felt that there wasn't much more that he could do. He warned my parents to prepare for the worst and told them, "The baby's intestines are working like a straight line from his mouth to his anus. Any food he eats goes straight through his system without little digestion."

My contact with the new baby remained limited, but when I did see him, I loved watching him curl up, like a little ball, against my mother with his plump, red, and peachy cheeks, and his dark, wavy hair.

In response to Irfan's illness, my mother became increasingly reclusive and spent all her waking hours observing him to make sure that he didn't take a turn for the worse. For her, that time became a nightmare in which she couldn't find relief, think about anything else, or even sleep.

During the course of this trying time, my father's older sister gave us some good news – she wanted us to join her in Texas, where she'd agreed to sponsor us for residency in the United States. My parents knew immediately that they wanted to move to America because they thought that this might give Irfan a better chance of surviving.

This worrisome time was also an exciting time; my older brothers talked excitedly about the plane ride and the cars we'd see once we arrived in America. Our last day in Karachi was unforgettable – with suitcases strewn about, my parents moved quickly, making sure they'd packed everything. I copied their movements and considered what I, at six years old, couldn't do without. Instinctively, I put my books, primarily my English and Urdu language books, in an open suitcase – the thought of forgetting what I'd learned from them filled me with great regret. I couldn't leave them.

"Why are all these books in this suitcase?" *Abba* asked pointing to the books.

"I'm taking them with us. I'll need them to remember what I've learned," I said.

"You won't need those anymore. We'll buy new books once you're in a new school," he explained.

"But they won't be the *same books*," I said sadly.

"I promise that you will like your new books, too," he said, patting me on the back.

Books weren't the only things being left behind. We had to leave my mother's family home, the house that my mother and aunt grew up in and the one that my brothers and I were all born into. The structure of that house appeared gigantic to my child's eyes; the main entrance had a large ascending staircase, which led to a second floor. There, an expansive veranda, opposite bedrooms, allowed the resident to look onto the city perimeter. Floors of cold stone absorbed burning light and strong concrete beams flowed upwards seemingly touching the sky. Like the other homes in the area, cement walls enclosed the house and kept the city, and its crime, at bay, giving us all a place of refuge.

My brothers and I loved exploring and playing in different parts of the house. I fought to be included in the fun because my brothers didn't like me holding them back, telling on them, or being a sissy in general, so, I tried to fit in. Sometimes I succeeded, sometimes I failed, but I couldn't sit around all day like other girls I'd see in school or at parties. Instead, I skipped and jumped to my heart's content. My brothers and I ran around, chasing each other, hiding, or climbing trees. It didn't matter whether we were at home or at a party with our parents – wherever the place, we would all burst into a sprint and start playing tag.

On hot days, everyone moved to the second floor to take naps. One afternoon while the adults napped, my brothers and I snuck downstairs. Though our grandfather forbade us from playing outside unattended, the plan was to do so anyway. An irritable man by nature, my grandfather often became angered by our antics. I didn't think about him that afternoon. Rather, I focused on the fact that I wasn't going to be left out like I had been the last time.

Today, I would help my brothers build a mud city. When tasks were being relegated, I realized that we had passed the point of no return. I carried spoons while Samir and Nasir carried buckets of water. We walked away from the kitchen and tip-toed towards the rear entrance of the house. At this juncture, focus was crucial, and we moved stealthily to avoid enemy detection. When we made it to the backyard, we dropped everything and surveyed the surroundings. The coast was clear. We sat underneath two open windows, a location difficult to see from inside the house.

When they ascertained safety, my brothers sat down and started to build their mud city. Water was mixed with mud, and construction began on time. Every few minutes, the jobs of architect and builder interchanged between them. I was assigned the task of making my own little town in the city outskirts.

"Go sit over there," Samir said.

"Make sure you're quick with the water. We need it back here soon," Nasir said.

Instead of delving into construction, I spent my time mixing mud with water, digging holes, and daydreaming.

We all played happily for some time, but then, someone started yelling. The shouts came from inside the house. A white undershirt and hair made a clear outline against the dark window frame above us and left no doubt as to who had been watching. Samir and Nasir looked at their city to see if they could salvage anything. As one of the side doors swung open, they gave each other a frantic look, and with quick movements, they sped away.

At five years old, I was confused as to what had just transpired, but I knew the situation terrified me and that I didn't want to be at the receiving end of all that shouting and yelling. I stood temporarily frozen. After a moment, I decided to run, but it was too late. My hesitation cost me crucial yards and the thin, tall man with wispy, white hair was in front of me within seconds. He shook my shoulders and yelled, "What do you think you're doing?"

As I looked up into my grandfather's face with its white beard and sharp features, I started crying. Frozen again, I couldn't speak. All of a sudden, something like regret flickered on his face, and his eyes became bigger as he raised his brow. His grip loosened. Perhaps he'd assessed that building a city in the backyard hadn't been my idea, and that the masterminds were on the run. It seemed as if he might reassure me, but then he looked into the distance, searching for my brothers. His face moved back into a frown. He forgot about me and ran after them. I took my chance and raced towards the house. Safely reaching the inside of the kitchen, I snuck up to the second floor, going into a bedroom and not daring to come out for the rest of the afternoon.

I wondered about my brothers. Had they found the right hiding place or had they been found out? Maybe they made it to my mother and hid behind her. Whatever the case, I'm still uncertain about what happened after my escape. If my brothers were caught, it must have been horrifying. Why did my grandfather scare me so much, and why was he so serious all the time? Though I didn't know it at the time, the answer could be found in his past.

Chapter 5
Other Immigrants
✹ ✹ ✹ ✹ ✹

My mother's father and mother were born in a time of great change and widespread global crisis. Lives were unpredictable and children were propelled into adulthood before their bodies could catch up. World War I came and passed, and then, fascism gained ground among people who had once believed in the primacy of reason, a people once touched by the Enlightenment. World War II gripped the globe during my grandparents' formative years while British Colonial Rule, entrenched in the Indian Subcontinent for hundreds of years, swayed and then collapsed completely.

Pakistan was created in 1947, two years after the end of World War II, and its birth was bloody – the creation of a border between India and Pakistan, better known as The Partition, involved the simple act of using a pen to make lines on a map, but the blood-letting that followed had incalculable consequences – Hindus, Muslims, and Sikhs who had lived together for centuries started creating complimentary boundaries in their hearts and minds. Hindus were pushed to one side of the border and Muslims to the other, with Sikhs believing in the sanctity of both religions, trying to find solid ground wherever they could.

My mother's parents were *Mohajirs*, or migrants who relocated from India to Pakistan during The Partition – they settled in Karachi, Pakistan's most populous city. No matter the spreading squalor within Karachi's new shanty towns, my grandparents built a secure home, located in Defense Housing Authority, one of the city's safest locations. Regardless of the security of this home, the instability of their times never allowed my mother's family complete relief. My grandfather warned my mother and aunt about good times saying,

"Don't become attached to good times because bad times are coming right after them."

For him, everything had always been tenuous. Rigorous responsibility was thrust onto my grandfather, Nazir Khan, or *Baba* as everyone called him, at twelve years of age, when his father succumbed to an unknown illness and became a recluse. After this point, my great-grandfather rarely interacted with his family to offer any support or guidance.

Instantly, *Baba* became the head of the household since his mother, like all other women of that society, was limited in what she could do. Females couldn't fathom thriving without a viable link to a man, and without this visible connection, a woman was considered suspect. Women needed the "guidance" of a male relative, even if that relative was a child. So *Baba* was given much authority, at a young age, and would continue to be the guardian of his mother and sisters for the rest of his life. In speaking of his mother, my grandfather said, "I've been a parent to my mother longer than she was ever a parent to me."

As a child, I saw them, my grandfather and great grandmother, speaking to each other a handful of times – she'd always look on lovingly while he stood with a more serious stance. When he left her company, she'd feel comfortable enough to pull out a small multicolored, tin box containing her favorite games and start playing solitaire. If her son happened to return after remembering one last point, she'd quickly hide everything back in the box.

Everyone called my great grandmother *Nani Ma*, meaning simply, grandma. All I know about her is that her ancestors may have migrated to South Asia from some other part of the world because her fair complexion and thin, long limbs were indicative of foreign blood. My grandfather shared the same complexion and stature.

Nani Ma was married off at fourteen, to a husband twice her age. Before her marriage, she'd usually spend the day sitting under the shade of tropical trees or running around, but after her marriage, she started dealing with the responsibilities of motherhood. From this point on, she became a servant of sorts because her husband held strong opinions regarding how children should be raised. He yelled at *Nani Ma* saying things like, "Feed him this way!" or "Don't put her clothes on like that!"

Nani Ma's marriage continued this way until her husband's death. From then on, she never wore anything besides a white *sari* as was expected of widows of her day, and in the limited memories I have of her, she's always wearing the same type of *sari*.

I had the opportunity to spend time with her before my family left for the United States. We'd both sit on the sofa, in the living room, with the smooth green carpet under our feet. She'd complain about her aches, pains, and especially her wrinkles. I told her that when I grew up, I'd become a doctor and find a way to fix her physical problems. I held her face between my hands and lifted her cheeks up saying, "You see, your wrinkles are gone. When I'm a doctor, I'll figure out how to fix your wrinkles for good," I said patting her on the back.

Impressed that a five-year-old child could think in such terms, *Nani Ma* told my mother that one day I'd, "Do something amazing like become a great doctor who would heal the world." What would *Nani Ma* think of me at twenty? What would she think of my achievements? I was no doctor, and my only goal was to attend my second year of college. Some greatness that was.

Unlike *Nani Ma*, my grandfather wasn't someone who gave compliments easily. In order to deal with his responsibilities and the uncertainties of life, he became singularly focused, becoming obsessed with his studies and then work. He finished his education and worked as a banking executive for the rest of his life. Though he excelled in his career, his life resembled that of an ascetic because indulging in pleasure wasn't part of his repertoire. Life wasn't meant for pleasure anyway, it was meant for self-sacrifice. Instead of splurging on food or drink, he'd eat just a *samosa* during the workday and, in this way, accumulated more money for his family. Due to his meager diet, he remained extremely thin throughout adulthood.

Bearing the weight of the world on his shoulders, he was constantly irritable. He'd often snap at his wife or children.

"Shut up you fools!" he often yelled at his daughters.

He lectured my mother and aunt about the centrality of work in an honorable life. "There's no other honor in life than an honest day's work. You girls like to waste your time. Forget about your foolish fantasies. This makeup, this fashion, this jewelry is all rubbish. I want you to become well-educated and stand on your own feet in this world, or else it will take everything from you. Bear the gravity of this world with the shield of education – people are fickle, but you can trust knowledge," he said.

As his daughters grew older, he found more nuanced ways to criticize what he thought of as questionable decisions. Writing a letter to my mother after we'd been living in the U.S. for a few years, my grandfather implored her to move back to Pakistan.

"Your children are not meeting their potential because of the difficulties that immigration has brought. Their education suffers every day you stay in America. Top quality schools are waiting for them in Karachi, so bring them back and salvage their education. In America, the best that they can hope for is to become mechanics." His letters always conveyed the importance of self-control, planning, and discipline.

Regardless of all the self-control though, my grandfather had a life-long vice – smoking cigarettes. Breathing problems related to cigarettes caused his death in 1988, but he probably passed away, without guilt, knowing that his whole life had been spent taking care of his mother, sisters, wife, and daughters.

My grandmother Azeema, or *Begum* as most called her, was a softer soul than my grandfather. She was not one to yell or lecture, but was a kind and loving parent. In her pictures, she always had her hair back in a bun and wore formal *saris*. She seemed to be assessing the world, looking onto it through her thick eye glasses. *Begum* had been greatly molded, at seven years of age, by the loss of her mother. For her deceased mother, she had an abundance of affection. Perhaps it was that child's desperation for the presence of her mother that made her memories so real, or maybe it was her memories that made her so desperate. Whatever the case may have been, her memories were something that she couldn't or wouldn't lose. Her mother would never be replaced.

Others didn't feel with the same intensity as *Begum* – her father remarried quickly after the death of his first wife. My grandmother would later recall her stepmother and say that, "that woman could never compare to my real mother." If any child could disown her parent, *Begum* did so with her father. Choosing to live on the second floor of her aunt's home, located right next to a graveyard, instead of living with her father, *Begum* created a distance and declared her continuing loyalty to her mother.

During her life, *Begum* put on many masks that disguised her desperation for love – she wore the mask of a humanitarian in the guise of a physician. In her day, the purpose of a woman's higher education, even in the West, was to secure a good marriage, but *Begum's* educational pursuits were not so singularly driven. She was also focused on work, like her husband, but her obsession went deeper than supporting her family. She'd craved the power to heal long before she went to medical school, and in becoming a doctor, she gained some control over her chaotic surroundings. It would be the control she didn't have when she'd wanted to stop her mother's death. So, she linked herself to universal suffering and became a balm to Karachi's suffering masses. In so doing, she joined the city's deluge of pain and perdition and became entangled in an endless circle of life, disease, and death.

Later in her life, *Begum* switched roles and took on the face of a cancer patient, recovering and then relapsing. Finally, the cancer metastasized. Debilitated, she must have had time to think, even though she was in great pain. She must have considered whether she had done everything she could have to help those who needed healing. Would her daughters, women without the protection of brothers, be able to deal with the trials of life? Luckily, she'd had the time to arrange my mother's marriage to a good man. He had kind eyes, and among the thousands of faces that she'd seen in her lifetime, she felt that his was one she could trust.

Perhaps, as she lay dying, she thought again about her own mother's death. Would her mother finally come back for her now that death approached her, or would she meet her mother on the other side of the curtain between life and death? As she considered these thoughts, the cancer destroyed organ, tendon, and bone. My grandparents' home had become quiet except for *Begum's* painful breathing. The sounds of what seemed to be a subdued drum thumped through the house as her lungs attempted inhalations and then collapsed in on themselves. With these sounds, my mother and aunt's dread and fear of disease solidified.

"*Inna Lillahi Wa Inna Ilayhi Raji Un,*" my grandfather said. The utterance of these words, "surely we belong to God

and to God we shall return", customarily uttered after someone passes away, confirmed to everyone that *Begum* had left
the world. It's been forty years since she died, but just like her
mother, she is not easy to forget.

Chapter 6
Priorities
※ ※ ※ ※ ※

My mother could have chosen to continue with my grandmother's legacy by devoting her life to Karachi's sick and suffering. With a combination of parental encouragement and natural talent, *Ammi* excelled academically and scored eleventh in a city-wide exam of high school students, after which time she entered and completed medical college. Despite her academic achievement though, my mother gave up her career to raise her children.

Even after her children became older, *Ammi* didn't want to work outside the home because it would mean spending less time with her children. Completely preoccupied with the kids, she was obsessed with what they needed and forgot about everything else. When we came home from school, she'd be waiting to find out how everyone was. Every day after school or college or work, depending on the years in question, *Ammi* would check in with everyone, especially Nasir and Irfan, who in childhood, were the habitually sick ones. They continued to receive extra attention into adulthood. She would ask, looking up expectantly, "How was your day, *beta*?"

"It was fine. I'm going to watch some TV now," Nasir answered.

"You're just getting over a fever. Are you sure you're okay?" *Ammi* asked as she felt Nasir's forehead.

"Uh-huh," he answered, turning on the TV.

"Okay, good. I have some chicken. Do you want to eat that for dinner?" she asked.

"Yes," he answered. Nasir didn't really hear my mother's last question because, by then, he was completely absorbed in the television show he'd just turned on.

My mother would then scurry to the kitchen and prepare dinner. She'd often want me to help in the kitchen, but I preferred going up to my bedroom to talk on the phone, read, or finish up homework.

Ammi longed for her children to have the same kind of life that she had as a child. This wish was idealistic but improbable. How could my parents, immigrants new to the rules and ways of America, provide the same kind of life to their children that my mother's extremely well-established parents had provided for her in her homeland?

So, my mother gave up part of the dream but remained passionate about keeping her children safe and healthy. Our physical health became her priority. After all the illnesses she'd witnessed, achievement and acclaim became negligible in her eyes. This was partly why it was difficult for her to understand my desire to leave home for college, but for me, there was no point to health if I couldn't live the way I wanted.

In high school, kids picked up on the fact that I had this single-minded focus on school and joked that being from Asia meant being a nerd, and maybe it was true in my case, but my culture couldn't have been the only reason I craved the return to college. So many people from the same part of the world I came from, young and old, worked full-time jobs at local fast-food places or convenience stores – they had forgotten all about education. I doubted that they had enough energy to take one class during the week, let alone pursue a degree.

Self-sacrifice was the difference between us – their lives centered on sublimation of the self, and my life centered on myself, at least for those four years in college. Feeling a combination of dread and awe, I watched them mustering will power to sacrifice for their families. In their fast-food worlds, they allowed their minds to waste, so they could contribute to the family income. Some even saved and sent money to their relatives overseas.

As I waited in line to buy a taco at one store or a burger at another, their hollow stares looked the same. Whether a customer talked down to them in disdain or tried to engage them in polite conversation, their response remained uniform.

"Would you like anything else with that order…thank you for shopping and come again."

Sometimes, customers lost control and snapped. One night, on the way home from working at Science Exploration,

I stopped at Taco Bell. I saw a middle-aged, male customer, in blue overalls, shouting at the Indian woman behind the counter. "Are you deaf or just stupid?" he shouted.

As I watched him, clearly overreacting to the woman's oversight, I suspected that he was not so much angry at the worker's mistake as he was reveling in his power over her. I realized that she'd never say anything in retaliation – this was her handicap, the handicap of need and necessity.

"I'm sorry sir," her Rs rolled, giving away her South Asian background.

"Don't say sorry, just don't be stupid!" he shouted.

"Why don't you give her a break?" I yelled without any trace of an accent.

Everyone behind the counter looked up in surprise. It felt heroic, in the instant that I defended her, but what I had just done sank in when the man turned around, and I suddenly noticed his size. He must have been six-two and at least a hundred pounds more than me. My body forced me to swallow, and I gulped. If words could have been weapons, we could have battled as equals, but this wasn't a court of law. Luckily, this man, this everyday bully, had not heard me clearly.

"What?" he asked.

"Nothing," I said and walked out the door.

As I walked away from the restaurant, my disgust for predatory behavior overwhelmed me. The brutality of the interaction I'd just witnessed showed me that there wasn't much that separated some human beings from animals; people also ganged up on and decimated individuals trapped in positions of weakness. Yes, in my opinion, the mean man in the restaurant was worse than a crocodile or shark.

I wouldn't give him the benefit of the doubt and immediately linked his inhumane treatment to discrimination. It made me shudder to think that I belonged to the group which aroused this kind of hatred in others. Like all the other immigrants before, South Asians were now newcomers, which meant that it was our turn for the worst. After all, hadn't the Chinese, Africans, Eastern Europeans, Jews, Irish, and Italians also experienced their share of bigotry? Weren't some of those groups still experiencing discrimination, even after being in the country for hundreds of years? This must be the way of this country, I thought to myself, because no matter how hard we work against it, in order for some to be on the inside, others would have to be left out.

While walking, my mind transported back to a place I wished to forget – I couldn't stop thinking about the bus rides I took to and from high school because they were my worst memory of high school. A group of bullies regularly ruined these rides for me, as well as for the rest of the students on the bus. Not particularly tall or muscular, the bullies looked like "regular" boys their age. Initially, I liked their hair color, which ranged from brown to blond and their light eyes of brown or green or blue, and before I knew them, I looked at these teenaged boys the way any teenaged girl would, with wonder and curiosity.

Over time, I'd realize more about them; they were average students, not attending the honors or advanced placement classes, but they were gifted in what they did – taunting, mocking, cursing, and the transference of mortification in the early mornings.

The bullies' intrusions into others' lives happened every day. The morning, which should have been the most hopeful time, became a dreaded one, and the bus always boomed with one threatening noise or another.

"Loooooooooooooser!" one of them would yell, growling like an animal, and then, they'd all burst into maniacal laughter. The first part of the taunt was meant to grab everyone's attention because "loser" could refer to anyone.

Woken out of morning drowsiness, my heart started to beat fast, Thump...thump...thump...

"Staaaaaaaaannnnnnn. Are you shaking? Are you afraid, *faggot*?" and again came the maniacal laughter.

Stan ignored them and continued reading. The only reaction he ever gave them was to turn around and look at them. Though the bullies looked down on him, I actually admired Stan and his studious, neat, and quiet manner. Over time, I came to hate those bullies, not just because of their loudness and obnoxiousness, but because they also had horrible taste. Everyone I liked, they looked down on, and anything that was uninteresting, loud, or annoying, they loved.

"Whaaat woooood you like with that, how bouuuttt a sluuurpie?" they laughed again.

I turned my head to see what they were doing. As usual, there was unending movement at the back of the bus. On the outside seats of the very last row, two of the bullies had their feet in the aisle. One of the boys made the *Nameste* sign to his friends, and the other acted like he was drinking something.

"Ayesha's dad is a loser, and he works at 7-11. He loves slurrpies because he's a dothead," they all laughed in unison. I could fight with my parents, or even tease them, but how dare these lowlifes bring up my father? I lost it.

"Racist assholes," I shouted

"What?" They were always surprised when I retaliated.

"You heard me, *fuck you*, you assholes!" I shouted again.

"Oooh, I'm so scared, the dothead is going fight us," one of the bullies said laughing.

"Yeah, we should fight. I bet I could beat you pieces of shit up," I went on.

After a few moments of silence, I continued, "Oh are you scared. Can't even fight a girl, huh?" I said.

As a teenager, I became so worked up that I no longer cared about the consequences, but at that moment, with indignation overwhelming me, I felt certain that I could give the bullies a good fight. I didn't like the way I reacted in these situations. I didn't recognize the loud and angry girl I became because, usually, I was a quiet conformist. But they were the ones that changed things and made everything ugly. Why couldn't they just leave everyone alone?

"Freeeeeeeaaaaaaaaaaaak," they growled again.

"Eilllllllllllleeeeeennn is a freak!"

Eileen – another example of someone I liked who they didn't. Eileen's family was Jewish, and I related to her because, like me, she always had a different take on things. She explained why those boys liked bullying.

"They yell and scream because they want to feel better about themselves. No one really likes them, and you don't know what goes on in their homes. Maybe their parents hate them too," Eileen said.

"Eillleeeeeeeennnnnn!"

I wanted to defend her, but she stopped me and said, "It's ok, there's always going to be someone around to try to fuck up your day. I'm used to it."

"We've had to deal with this shit for way too long. I think I'm going to talk to the principal," I said.

"Do you think that will really change anything?" Eileen asked.

"I don't know, but I want to do something," I said.

I did complain about the bus rides to the principal's office. Why should I have had any loyalty to those boys? I didn't care if they told the whole school that I ran to the principal to tattle. I didn't fear them because it felt like their abuse had already damaged something in my being, the part of my psyche that wanted to be accepted, to be loved and part of the whole, to be liked by boys and to be thought of as nice and pretty by them; after those things were damaged, what more could they take away?

The principal took the matter seriously and asked for the names of the boys causing problems. As I said their names, I realized that I, who had been powerless for so long, now had some power. I left that office feeling good about my decision.

Action was taken quickly, and the status quo finally changed. The group no longer screamed or taunted on the bus, at least for a few months, but this controlled behavior didn't last indefinitely – towards the end of the school year, their taunting started again, but by that time, summer vacation was only a few weeks away. The next year, they no longer took the bus, and I never had to share a bus ride with them again.

A few years after high school though, someone drew a swastika, in chalk, in front of my parent's home. Was the fact that the swastika was drawn in chalk supposed to take away from its seriousness? No matter what material was used to draw it, that symbol could not be disconnected from hatred and inhuman violence. Its use always conveyed that a certain type of evil still existed – one fueled by ignorance that aimed to damage human life for no other reason than to cause destruction.

A police report was created, but the identity of the individual or individuals responsible couldn't' be ascertained. Could the same boys who had bothered me be responsible for the drawing? No one can say for sure, but the sentiment in the action certainly had a similar feel to the abuse a lot of us went through on those bus rides.

Escaping bullies, like the ones on that bus, was one of the reasons that a women's college proved to be a welcome relief. During my time at Chestnut Hill College, I never experienced open taunting or name calling. I found that the women in college rarely mocked others openly and preferred quiet subterfuge, like in freshman year, when my friend and classmate privately told our professor that I shouldn't have received a higher grade on my paper than she did on hers because she'd worked on her paper all week, whereas I'd only devoted a day's work on mine. She went onto tell the professor that I didn't like one of the particular classes she'd taught that semester, and that, one evening, I'd gone to the extent of imitating her lecture for laughs. Taken out of context, it could be assumed that I didn't like that professor, but the truth was, at that time, she was actually my favorite professor. In this case, imitation really had been the sincerest form of flattery. What my friend did was damaging, but it was motivated by pettiness and insecurity, not intolerance, and somehow, these justifications for bad behavior were easier for me to deal with than mocking or name-calling from males.

Overall, immersion into the college environment was a welcome change. It was part of the goals of the college to welcome and guide all students in the community – the mission of the college was based on the philosophy of the Sisters of Saint Joseph, a philosophy centered on service. The students may not have always liked or supported each other, but the sisters and professors tried their best to. As a student at Chestnut Hill College, I found the professors and employees' attempts to guide me endearing, and it was ironic that I, as a Muslim woman, found a sanctuary of learning and belonging among a community that had religious beliefs and rituals so different than my own. It convinced me that human beings, no matter their backgrounds or what the forces of division had to say, could thrive together.

And finally, here was a place where your effort counted. Professors genuinely cared about your work. Even when you failed, professors tried to help you succeed. One afternoon, I sat in a course for The Interdisciplinary Scholar's Program, the honors program at Chestnut Hill College, which I'd been invited to join in my first semester at college. The course, focused on studying the intersection between society and architecture, had proved to be fascinating. I admired the easy way that Professors Kitchen and Conway interacted with each other in class to deliver their expertise on the subject matter. Class was about to start, so I pulled out my notebook. The professors said they had an announcement.

"Before we start class, we have to discuss the papers that were handed in last week; unfortunately, the papers, with the exception of one or two, did not meet the caliber of what is expected in the honor's program. We are handing the papers back with the expectation that they will be revised within a week," Professor Conway said.

I couldn't understand what had happened. I'd devoted so much time working on that paper. I couldn't look the professors in the eye. Maybe I couldn't succeed in academics, just like I might not succeed anywhere. I waited to see what they wrote on my paper, and after it was in my hand, I flipped through the first few pages. There were a lot of notes from the professors. Flipping to the last page, I braced myself to find out if I'd gotten a D or an F. To my surprise, the grade was an A. Relief washed over me. I looked up thankfully towards the professors and received a knowing look in return. The fact that I was one of the only two students to receive a good grade made me realize that academics were the ones who consistently welcomed me into their world; unlike other places, I was never left out in academia as long as I tried my best.

Other professors also helped me to become more confident. Sister Mary Helen, the director of the French Department, transferred to me a drop of the ocean that was her knowledge. Extremely well read on history and a polyglot on top of that, she was the epitome of intelligence; Sister Mary Helen was someone who learned just for the love of learning. After years of practice, her Russian and French were perfect. One day, I asked Sister Mary Helen what she thought about me majoring in French.

"English is not your first language. Do you realize that your brain is hardwired to incorporate a diversity of languages into your lexicon? So, of course you can major in French. I have no doubt that with your focus, you'll be able to succeed," she said.

I was moved by her comment – it meant so much coming from someone as learned as her. Sister Mary Helen's support and the support of others like her was why I had fought to go to college and why I fought to stay there.

Just like Sister Mary Helen, I loved learning, and I also didn't see learning just as a means to end. I had other reasons for wanting to finish my education, besides putting a degree on a resume. Why did learning have to become so entwined with what came afterwards anyway? Couldn't we simply learn for the love of it? As class lessons and life intertwined, I wondered what the men and women I studied in history books would think about the way schooling worked in the United States towards the end of the twentieth century. What would the minds of the European Enlightenment have to say about the fact that we now went to school so we could put a degree on our resumes? What would Montesquieu or Olympe de Gouges have to say?

Before these thinkers, the French were a confused people, not knowing which path to choose, but when the great minds of that generation appealed to learning and reason, France changed. The French called their experience *Le siècle des Lumières*, literally meaning the century of lights. They found their brightening, not with war or domination, but through the multiplying light that emanates from knowledge. This was their enlightenment.

In college, I worked towards my own enlightenment, as the century came to a close and a new millennium emerged on the horizon. I sought understanding in the midst of change. The college walls were a refuge where the interplay of minds was primary, and where discussions, debates, and diversions revolved around thought, philosophy, and emotion. Individual students were wrapped up in their own epiphanies while I struggled to find truth and the words by which I could describe its discovery – I wanted lessons that would lead me to a longed for illumination when *everything* would finally make sense. If it happened to the French, then maybe it could happen to me, and that destination was the one I desired the most.

But wanting something doesn't necessarily mean that you attain it and, sometimes, all the help in the world can't move you where you need to be. For me, and others like me, pursuing a college degree was not easy. Nevertheless, being on campus helped me wage a war for my future.

Chapter 7
Living
✹ ✹ ✹ ✹ ✹

I couldn't compare that first year at Chestnut Hill to anything that came before or after, but I almost missed my chance of starting college that semester. By the time I let the college know whether I'd be attending in the fall of 1997, there weren't any rooms left in Fontbonne, the freshmen dorm. After being assigned to the upper-classmen dorm, Saint Joseph's Hall, I moved in, joining a small number of seniors, juniors, sophomores, and other freshman already there.

Students lived on the fourth floor; the fifth floor housed science labs and the main art studio, situated in the center of the hall next to the rotunda. Science labs lined a peripheral hallway. Various scientific paraphernalia were visible in illuminated glass cases – imitation human skulls, tools for dissection, thermometers, and test tubes were displayed neatly on shelves. Wandering around on the fifth floor without reason wasn't permitted, but after hours, that is precisely what my newly found friends and I did.

Nighttime at Saint Joseph's Hall became the most exciting part of the day as we previewed student artwork and peered into science labs. I don't know what we thought we'd find there, and I don't know what the others observed, but I discovered dim hallways filled with a certain resonance and a subtle energy left by the day.

Aliya, Julie, Kim, and Jen were my Saint Joe's buddies. All from honest and hard-working families, their openness to those different than themselves mirrored their good upbringing.

Aliya and I graduated from North Penn High School together and then started attending Chestnut Hill College after high school. Aliya's room was close to mine, and, in the evenings, I'd take a break from homework and shuffle over to her room, in my slippers and pajamas, to talk to her.

"Remember when Mrs. Staley had us act out Hamlet in English class. I still remember my lines. To be or not to be, that is the question, Aliya. Isn't Dr. Lonnquist brilliant by the way? Her short stories class is so awesome," I said.

"Oh Ayesha, we're biology majors now. Let's start focusing on biology. DNA isn't going to magically make sense to us unless we study," she said with a smile. Aliya often said logical things but followed what she said with a smile – that friendly smile, in combination with the fact that she had amusing insights about life, made her someone that always drew friends.

"Don't be mad, Aliya, but I don't know if I want to continue with biology. There's languages, there's literature, there's sociology. I'll see how I feel next semester," I said.

"Oh, Ayesha, please make up your mind," Aliya said.

At Saint Joe's, Kim and Julie would figure out what our group did in the evenings, and I'd decide whether I wanted to join or head over to Fontbonne Hall to hang out with my other friends. When I stayed, the group had conversations till all hours of the night, watched movies, and told ghost stories.

We'd gather in the hall lounge, when the nights were particularly quiet and ominous. One evening, we sat in the lounge and waited for a sign to see what we should do next. We could tell that something in between the moon-laden sky and howling wind was watching us – yes, something strange conveyed its presence in the ether.

With her hair tied back in a bun and her dark eyes aglow amidst her tanned, brown skin, Kim relayed some of the rumors that still circulated about Saint Joseph's Hall. Kim's father was from Jamaica, so she had a knack for knowing about extraordinary things. Kim grew up listening to Jamaican legends of the supernatural and was able to make connections about the believability of surrounding stories that we could not.

Preparing myself, I sank back into my seat on the sofa. Only one of the lights was on; it reflected off of different surfaces in the lounge. The room was filled with the type of furniture you'd find in a country cottage, like sofas with checkered patterns of large red, green, and brown stripes. It was also the type of furniture you'd see people sitting on, in a horror movie, right before the killer showed up. I jumped as the old metal radiators tapped wildly behind us.

With the five of us present, we felt safe enough to hear what was about to be said. We all moved to the floor to listen more intently to what Kim had to say. She spoke in a whisper,

"There have been deaths here, suicides that we haven't heard about."

"Why wouldn't we know about them, why wouldn't someone tell us?" I asked, urging her to continue.

"Think about it. Why would they tell us something like that? If they were going to tell us that, then they might as well tell us that this campus is haunted and dangerous. *It is true* that a woman lived here a long time ago. She went about her life here, doing her duties, and one day, a day like any other, she just threw herself off the rotunda. Some say it could have been a demonic possession of a pure soul. Keep your ears open late nights, and you will hear her waking out of eternal sleep because she still wants to make her footsteps heard through these echoing halls. Perhaps she was forced to witness something unbearable, like an event or events that made her so still that she had to take her own life, ended quickly in suicide. Never doubt that she still walks here, or she may have to reveal herself to you."

"Whoa," we all said, looking at each other and shaking our heads.

That night, Kim's story freaked us all out, but the feeling passed the next day. Supernatural dangers were one thing, but what about the other dangers that I had to worry about, like the ones my mother warned me about, kidnapping and murder.

At night, when I worked at Logue Library, sometimes even until ten o'clock, my mother felt extremely anxious about my safety, sometimes making multiple calls to check in on me. She didn't understand why I worked so late because a young woman working by herself, at night, was unheard of where she grew up. So, in order to maintain my job, I asked Sister Mary Jo if someone from the staff could walk me to the door of the main building every night after work ended. The main building was only thirty feet from the library, but having someone walk with me made my mother feel better. Every night, one of the library's staff members, either Sister Mary Jo, Marian, Gail, or Carol, would walk me towards Saint Joseph's hall. I thought they might all think that the request to accompany me was weird, and I also felt bad that the staff had to stay with me for an extended amount of time, even if it was for a minute or two. Nevertheless, there was no judgment, and Sister Mary Jo,

Marian, Gail, and Carol all made me feel like I was family and not just a student who worked for them.

After I returned to my dorm, my mother would call me.

"Ayesha, have you locked your room?" she asked.

"Yes, it's locked, and there's no one here, anyway," I said.

"Are you sure that visitors aren't allowed on campus at night?" she asked.

"The only non-students on campus right now are the security guards," I said.

"You still have to be careful. There's been many cases where women have been abducted or gone missing, and no one knows where they are," my mom warned.

"That's scary. What cases?" I asked.

"Just read a newspaper. It happens all the time. That is why you have to stay safe by paying attention to your surroundings," my mother said.

"Okay, I will, I promise. *Ghuda Hafiz*," I said.

"*Ghuda Hafiz*," my mother said.

After hanging up with me, my mother let my father know that I was safe. They were both terrified of losing me in a land where they'd already lost so much.

After talking to my mother that night, my eyes darted back and forth, in the dark, as I wondered how women could go missing without any clues as to what had happened to them. The fact that people sometimes just disappeared horrified me, for myself and others, so I found myself giving my college friends the same lessons in caution that my parents gave to me. I irritated friends when I gave them safety suggestions or a word of warning over upcoming life choices. I thought these snippets of information invaluable, but others didn't agree. My next door neighbor, freshman year, had to put up with my advice all the time.

"Hey, I'm going out on a date tonight, so I won't be able to eat dinner with you," Nalani said.

"That's fine. Just be careful. You know there are a lot of criminals out there. How much do you really know about your date? You can't even tell, these days, if someone is a serial killer," I said.

"He's not a serial killer, and I'm a big girl, Ayesha," Nalani said.

"Ok, I'm just telling you because I want you to be safe?"
I said.

"Enough, Ayesha, I'll be fine," Nalani said.

"Just be safe," I said, satisfied that I had the last word.

Nagging my classmates paid off one winter night, when I rescued three women, myself included, from a potentially dangerous situation.

With hardly any signs of life, the chill made the all-girls campus even more quiet than usual. Glowing brass chandeliers illuminated dark hallways and offered welcome pockets of light among the surrounding shadows. Sitting in my room in Saint Joseph's Hall, I read the following week's assignments. *The Awakening* was due for Monday's literature class, and so far, the book was living up to its powerful title. I read on, so I could discuss the assignment in detail:

> *In short, Mrs. Pontellier was beginning to realize her position in the universe as a human being, and to recognize her relations as an individual to the world within and about her. This may seem like a ponderous weight of wisdom to descend upon the soul of a young woman of twenty-eight…but the beginning of things, of a world especially, is necessarily vague, tangled, chaotic, and exceedingly disturbing. How few of us ever emerge from such beginning! How many souls perish in its tumult! The voice of the sea is seductive; never ceasing, whispering, clamoring, murmuring, inviting the soul to wander for a spell in abysses of solitude; to lose itself in mazes of inward contemplation. The voice of the sea speaks to the soul. The touch of the sea is sensuous, enfolding the body in its soft, close embrace.*

As meal time drew close, I put down the book and walked towards the window, standing nearly six-feet high. Its frames, made of darkly stained wood, kept the room dry during the winter. Difficult to open, the iron hinges squeaked when the frames and the thick glass between them moved in either direction.

These buildings may have been quiet on weekends, but they served as silent witnesses to the dreams and fears of thousands who had come before me. Even among the quiet, the presence of people and their personas, physically long gone, still lingered so that you never felt completely alone.

The view from my room overlooked one of the college's court yards. Wrapping around the interior of the courtyard in a circle, Saint Joseph's main hallway had large windows lined up one next to the other. Winding through that hallway to walk to class, you could stop to look out into the winter with its gleaming-white reflection of ice and snow.

On that night, as I looked out into the winter twilight, I searched for students, walking in Saint Joseph's Hallway. I focused as I recognized the faces of friends or acquaintances, wrapped up in their own thoughts and oblivious to the fact that they were being watched. Some students walked lazily towards the cafeteria in their sweat suits while others conversed with each other.

Moving away from the window, I came back to my desk and prepared to take the walk to the cafeteria. Dinner at Chestnut Hill College could be entertaining or uneventful, depending on the company. I called my friend Molly to confirm our dinner plans.

"What are you doing for dinner tonight?"

"I'll meet you in front of the cafeteria in ten minutes, hummus," she said, using the nickname she'd given me.

"Okay great! I'll see you there."

I met Molly in the first class that I ever attended at Chestnut Hill College. In class, I noticed her straight red hair, blue eyes, and fair skin that turned bright red when something moved her. In class, she wasn't the most vocal in expressing her opinions and seemed to be the type more interested in absorbing what others said, but she spoke much more decisively in one-on-one conversation.

Distinct as a dresser, her outfits matched her two specific personas. While attending classes or meeting with a professor, Molly wore a blazer indicating her serious slant towards the moment. When she wasn't in class, her outfits were much more relaxed, which mirrored her more quiet and sensitive side. No matter the outfit, Molly always had a pen in hand, writing or moving it about. If the pen had a cap, then she'd constantly fidget with it. If it was the type of pen with a button, she'd endlessly click the pen open and then close it. She was the first real writer I'd ever met, and at eighteen, she already took her writing seriously.

"I have to write. I have to have others read my writing. I have to publish. Otherwise, after I die, there won't be anything left of me," she said.

"I do think there is another part of us that does go on. I think there's a soul," I said, becoming mesmerized by the idea that somewhere, inside every person, a spirit resided.

"You know I don't believe in that, Ayesha," she said.

"Yes, I'm sorry, I forgot. I guess I need to imagine you living on, somehow, if you talk about dying. I shouldn't have brought that up, but I think that others *will* read your work, and you *will* be remembered. You are very talented."

Over time, Molly convinced me that writing did offer a resurrection to writers every time their creative work was accessed and that the written word was a way to leave a part of yourself, in the world, after you departed. Years later, after nearing a psychological death of sorts, I started writing to let others know about my past and to declare, to scream even, before it was too late, that I had been here. Yes, I had lived, I had seen, and I had yearned. I was comforted by the idea that another human being could read what I wrote, even after I passed away.

"Hello there," I said, excited to see Molly in front of the cafeteria.

"Hiya," Molly said.

Taking our seats at a cafeteria table, Molly and I watched as the small remnants of the campus walked in. We saw Lana, a Bosnian exchange student, enter the cafeteria. Her pretty black curls bounced as she walked towards the dinner line. As always, her big brown eyes conveyed intensity as well as a certain depth of character. Freshman year, Lana worked hard and absorbed all the experiences a new country had to offer. That night, she picked out her dinner and took a seat across from us. She asked, "Do you guys want to do something off-campus after dinner?"

Molly and I both shook our heads yes. On that night, we would probably have agreed to fly to the Moon if the opportunity presented itself. And, yes, this seemed the night for something new and an evening to prove that women at a girl's college could also have adventures. Tonight, Molly, Lana, and I wanted an escape from the ordinary. Molly responded to Lana's question by saying,

"You mean, should we go off-campus after we regurgitate dinner?"

"Definitely slim pickings tonight," I said in agreement.

Lana giggled at our criticism of the cafeteria food.

"Well, is there anywhere we can go? I asked.

Do you mind if we drive somewhere Molly? Lana asked.

"Sure, should we go to Plymouth Meeting Mall?" Molly asked.

"Wait..wait…wait! I know what we should do. We should go to Atlantic City," I said.

Lana and Molly both looked at me approvingly.

"You are a genius, hummy!" Molly said and smiled.

We finished dinner quickly and, afterwards, scurried to our dorm rooms to pick up the essentials – wallets, coats, and hats.

"Who says we never have fun around here?" I asked.

"Go, go – hurry and pick up your wallet and coat," Lana said, waving her hands towards my dorm room. After we'd all collected our things, we ran towards the main entrance.

In the wintertime, the campus remained hot because the radiators always stayed on, so walking out into the fresh, cold air proved to be a welcome relief. I relished the cold on my skin.

We walked to Molly's car, an old station wagon handed down to her from her family, and when she unlocked the car, we made our way inside. Starting our trip, we soon reached the highway. Lana and Molly sorted out directions in the front, as I watched the highway lampposts. The car sped on, and the force of the tires made sounds on the concrete underneath.

We enjoyed talking to each other during the ride, but right before we reached our destination, the topic of sex suddenly came up. Molly asked Lana a very personal question, "Lana, have you ever…?"

Wishing to save her any embarrassment, I quickly answered for Lana.

"No, she never has because she's Muslim, and Muslims aren't allowed to do whatever you're about to ask. Plus, I don't want to talk about sex all the time. Isn't there anything else we can discuss? Now that I think about it, my parents would be so mad if they knew the topic of this discussion. Don't you have any self-control?" I asked sarcastically.

Molly became irritated and said, "Shut up, Ayesha. I wasn't asking you."

"I have done it," Lana said, shocking us both.

Molly laughed and said,

"You see that – people in your religion have sex too, even before they're married!"

"Remember what we learned about being culturally relative, Molly? I have a right to believe what I believe, and you have a right to your opinion. Besides, aren't you afraid of being used by men?" I asked.

"Men use women all the time. Why shouldn't we use them? I thought you were a feminist, Ayesha, but you're actually a prude. I'm sorry that Sister Pat ever brought up cultural relativism around you. I bet you're going to die alone," Molly said.

"At least I'll die with my self-respect. I am a feminist, but just because men do something stupid doesn't mean that women have to copy them. Women can't use men, anyway. It doesn't work like that. They aren't the ones that end up emotionally attached or pregnant. Now that we're on the topic though, you better watch yourself, Molly. What if you have sex and get pregnant? What would your parents think?" I said, realizing that I was repeating every word that my own parents had said to me on the subject.

"You're an idiot, Ayesha," Molly said.

Our conversation in the car that night was part of a larger, ongoing, and heated debate between us, regarding life and religion. It was natural for us to debate or argue because I was, at that stage in my life, quite religious while Molly was an atheist. Nevertheless, it was ironic that Molly, who wasn't religious, so loved the company of a Muslim woman, from a conservative Pakistani background, and a Bosnian-exchange student who came from a place where your religion could cost you your life.

Soon after our sex talk, we reached Atlantic City. Assaulted by the freezing ocean air, we ran into the closest casino. Once inside, we admired the interior, walking in the hallways and hotel areas. Not allowed to go into the actual casino where gambling took place, we walked around the periphery and admired the multicolored lights and patterns. Hungry again by this point, we sat down and had snacks in the café. For the rest of the night, we went from casino to casino, observing the differences between them.

Deciding to brave the cold, we walked towards the beach. The black water stood out against radiant sand, reflecting the white moon overhead. White foam from waves broke up the dark and periodically crashed into the beach.

I jumped up and down to keep myself warm, and these movements, which appeared silly, made the other girls laugh. I sprinted back and forth, partly to encourage more laughing, but mostly to warm myself. Once in a while, someone would shout "I'm freezing!" while the rest of us laughed. We continued on the beach, but by three-thirty in the morning, frozen and exhausted, we admitted that we couldn't go on.

"What are we going to do now?" I asked Molly.

"Umm…I'm too tired to drive home," she said

"How much would a motel room be?" I asked.

"Something like sixty to a hundred dollars, I think," Molly said.

"That's a lot of money. I can't afford that. Let's drink some coffee and drive back to college," I said.

"We should find a motel to stay in. We won't make it home if I have to drive right now," Molly continued.

"I can't afford it. It's too much money, even if we split it three ways," I said.

"I paid for the gas to come up to Atlantic City, cheapo," Molly said.

I'm not sure which one of us suggested it, but the idea of sleeping in Molly's car took root. The car was already parked in a lot after all. It wasn't ideal, but we could sleep a few hours and head back to the campus at first light.

We made our way back to the car. Using available blankets, make-shift beds were made in the front, middle, and back of the station wagon. Molly pulled back the driver's seat and covered herself with a blanket to minimize the freezing cold. Lana made herself comfortable in center of the station wagon, and I spread out in the back.

"It's so cold, Molly. Could you turn on the heat?" I asked

She let the heat run, but the air came out cold.

I started complaining "I can't believe I'm sleeping in a car. This sucks and, on top of that, it's freezing."

"Well, we don't have any other options right now. We can't do anything about it," Molly said.

I suddenly became suspicious. Three women sleeping in a car parked in Atlantic City screamed of adventure. Was she really too tired to drive back, or was she somehow inspired by this strange moment. Was sleeping in the car just good writing material for her?

Upset, I looked outside the car to focus on something else. Suddenly, I noticed something we'd all missed, on the brick wall behind us, the painting of a larger-than-life representation of a blond woman. Lips covered with bright lipstick, she had a wide smile on her face. Her breasts popped out of a red dress. She was clearly an advertisement for something inside the building.

"Oh my God, you guys, I think we're sleeping next to a strip club or sex club or something!" I shouted.

"What? How do you know?" Lana asked.

"Look over there," I said pointing.

"Damn," Molly said irritated.

I waited for the car to start so we could leave the parking lot, but to my surprise Molly didn't do anything. I imagined what my parents would say in this situation, and I could hear their voices in my mind.

"Our daughter walks on the wrong roads. She likes to wander around strange cities and sleep in station wagons. She likes to sleep near strip clubs."

My complaints intensified, and as I continued to freak out, a grey car pulled up next to us. In the car, two seemingly massive men stepped out, laughing and joking with each other. They wore sweat shirts and had shaved heads.

"Please don't let them see us. Please don't let them see us," I prayed.

But it was difficult to miss us. They stared into the car with a sense of entitlement that scared me. Glancing inside, they probably wondered what three women were doing, sleeping in the parking lot of a strip club. They exchanged puzzled looks and walked hesitantly towards their destination. The presence of these men sent me over the edge, and I started to lose my temper. My mother's voice started echoing more loudly in my mind.

"Guard your life, in this new land, or you could lose it," she said.

"Molly! Put the keys in the ignition and drive away now!" I yelled.

"Maybe we really should leave," Lana said.

As we argued, the two men were now walking quickly back to us. Luckily, the car doors were locked because we had had at least that much foresight. Although Molly had first been reluctant, she started to move more quickly.

By this point, the men reached their car, and one of them searched through the glove compartment while the other one opened the trunk. What were they looking for in the car? A knife? A gun? Would they really do something to us, or were they just trying to scare us for fun? Whatever the case may have been, we all ended up terrified and intimidated that night.

I focused fully on Molly. Would she maintain her where-withal and drive, or would she be paralyzed by fear? I couldn't take my eyes off her. Molly finally backed out of the parking space when Lana suddenly yelled "drive Molly, drive!"

Lana had seen the men doing something that neither Molly nor I had. When we were back on the highway, I asked Lana what happened, and why she was so scared?"

Shaken up, Lana said that she didn't want to talk about it in detail yet. Although she later told Molly exactly what had scared her so badly, she never talked about it with me again. Perhaps Lana and Molly thought I couldn't handle what Lana had seen, and that I'd become even more neurotic about the opposite sex if I knew what had happened. Whatever those men had done, whether it was gesturing or even showing a weapon, it had badly scared both of my friends.

Molly remembered, as we were driving away from the parking lot, that one of her aunts lived within half an hour of

Atlantic City. We decided to try to make it to her house, but after the night we had, who could tell whether we would arrive there in one piece.

Luckily, we made it there in spite of the exhaustion. When Molly parked the car, we all felt relieved. Since it was a vacation home, no one was inside the house to let us in, so we were back to sleeping in the car. After we parked in the driveway, Molly and Lana closed their eyes. I don't know how well they slept for the few hours we stayed there. I couldn't sleep fully because I kept shivering, but I might have slept for an hour.

Looking through the back of the station wagon, I kept a vigil to make sure that danger didn't crop up again. Molly's aunt's house was a small, one-story house, with a chain-linked fence around the yard, and I wanted so badly to be inside that little home, safe and warm. The surrounding water made the neighborhood windy, and you could see gusts of air hitting the house's pale, blue siding.

No question remained in my mind then. I knew that that evening must have been divine retribution for something I'd done, maybe punishment for leaving the college campus to go to Atlantic City without telling my parents, but whatever the reason, the night had really been hell. As if my thoughts were heard from a force outside of me, the dawn started to break. The sun would soon change things. It would make light what was dark and make warm what was once freezing. At that moment, what else could the sun coming up be but a sign of redemption? Within an hour, the life generating light of the sun started to overcome the night. Lana and Molly started stirring, and then opened their eyes. Our fear dissipated as everything around us became visible. We'd survived a cold, uncomfortable, and hellish night where violence could have ended us. In my mind, we would always be linked to each other after that night. We had all worked together, and our cooperation had saved us from possible danger and violence.

"Hey," Molly said to Lana and me.

"Good morning," we both returned.

She started the engine and drove to a nearby convenience store. Breakfast, coffee, and human interaction with the convenience store clerk was a welcome relief. Even though we were relieved, we were also all irritable because we blamed each other for what had happened the previous night. Molly and Lana could blame me for being cheap, and I could blame them for not moving the car as quickly as I had wanted.

Either way, we all decided to drive home quietly. I felt lucky when I saw the orange colored roofs of Chestnut Hill College. If things had gone differently the previous night, we may never have seen the campus again. We may have disappeared and subsequently hidden in some remote, makeshift grave like those women my mother always warned me about, but it hadn't happened that way. I was the reason that we had been in Atlantic City, but I may also have been part of the reason that we survived and returned to college in one piece.

We walked up to the main building, and upon reaching Fournier Hall, Molly and Lana headed towards their dorm while I walked back to Saint Joseph's – moving like a zombie through multiple hallways, I walked back to my dorm and used the elevator to make it to the fourth floor. Running to my room, I barricaded myself inside, and after I locked the door, I finally felt safe. Knowing that the world was now on the outside, I sensed a welcomed peace permeate my mind. I closed the plastic shutter that covered the dorm-room window and relished in the simple fact that I could turn the desk lamp on and off as I pleased. I left it on and enjoyed its subdued light before I threw myself into bed. Covering myself under the warm comforter, I adjusted my sheets and pillow. The old-style radiators started clicking loudly, like they usually did, but I didn't mind them this morning because they'd made the room deliciously warm. Doubting whether I was actually back in my room, I reached out my hand to feel the wall. I wanted to make sure that I wasn't still in Molly's car, dreaming of Saint Joseph's Hall. Realizing that I was definitely home, I became grateful for the things I had because they were things that not all people were assured.

Chapter 8
Conformity

✵ ✵ ✵ ✵ ✵

During my first year of college, I belonged to a community where my peers spent time with me, and even liked me. I'd occasionally be left out of things, like Molly and Lana's conversation about what really happened in Atlantic City, but on the whole, I belonged.

Yet I'll never be able to forget earlier years. The awkward and lonely girl I'd been had longed for this kind of acceptance. Until college, I'd never fully fit in. With the way other children acted around me, you'd have thought I had a disease. I didn't act or think like most other kids. I started to rebel against attempts at trying to "help me fit in." Perhaps other kids feared my individuality and my unwillingness to do exactly what everyone else did. Maybe it angered them that I felt entitled to act like myself when everyone else had to work hard to fit in.

My isolation may have been most pronounced from fifth grade to seventh grade when I left one school to be introduced to an entirely new one. My family moved to Conshohocken, Pennsylvania, a suburb of Philadelphia.

Seeing my new school for the first time made me hopeful for the future. On all sides of the central building, expansive fields covered everywhere the eye could see, and the only items that broke up the continuity were basketball courts and swing sets. During warmer weather, green grass would spread over everything, but in the winter, everything was frozen earth.

The exterior of the main building was typical for a public school – the outside walls were made of simple orange brick. Seemingly harmless, the outside of the building and its appearance never braced me for the little hooligans running amuck inside.

While attending school there, I felt the most powerless I ever had in my life because I was alone, confused, and unsure of what my future would hold. There wasn't anyone to spend time with except, maybe, some of the teachers who liked me.

My inability to pick up on social queues made others laugh, but being laughed at, although it wasn't ideal, wasn't as bad as being ignored completely. I talked of being from Pakistan all the time, disregarding the fact that my classmates didn't want to know or care about Pakistan.

"Pakistan is next to India on one side and next to Iran on the other," I said.

"Who cares about that?" someone would say to which the other kids would start laughing.

"Well, don't you think geography is fun?" I asked.

"Yeah, but who really wants to know where you're from?" another kid asked.

I told myself that they were laughing with me, not at me.

"Did you know I can speak Urdu?" I asked.

"What do you speak? Urdud?" another kid in the group asked.

Though I ignored the insults outwardly, the school created hopelessness in me. All that remains in my memory of middle school is a succession of uncomfortable and embarrassing events.

One source of embarrassment included irritating my English teacher, Mr. Morgan. Though he looked a little like sweet and friendly Mr. Rogers from PBS, always well-dressed, wearing button-down shirts, ironed pants and ties, his curly salt and pepper hair always combed and parted properly, Mr. Morgan was nothing like Mr. Rogers. Something about me drove him crazy. Perhaps he thought that I was what was wrong with the world – confusion, inefficiency, and emotionality all wrapped up in one annoying girl. When he spoke to me, his face turned red. Having formed strong opinions regarding English and education, he wanted everyone to have a perfect command of the language even, and perhaps especially, if English wasn't your first language. My mistakes not only bothered him but seemed to disgust him. As a child, it wasn't easy to distinguish whether he felt disgust for me or for my mistakes. To this day, I still don't know the answer to that question.

Reprimanding me in front of the class, he'd say things like "Ayeeeesha doesn't want to understand this lesson. She doesn't want to put in effort. Maybe she thinks she doesn't need to learn English properly. I don't know where you last went to school, but, in this school, we speak proper English."

I doubted if he would ever change how he felt about me, so I dreaded Mr. Morgan's presence – he inspired nothing but fear.

In addition to Mr. Morgan, my peers also didn't seem to like me. One afternoon during recess, a group of children stood in a circle and shouted. Walking up and joining them, I noticed everyone pointing to a slimy piece of rubber on the ground – it looked like a latex glove made for one large finger. I had a vague idea of what the object was and what it was used for. By the way the other children groaned at it, it must have been something horrible. Boys used sticks to lift and throw the plastic into the air while everyone else laughed and shouted. They'd balance the plastic on their sticks and go up to someone in the circle, bringing the plastic uncomfortably close to the victim's face.

My homeroom classmate, Judy, stood in the crowd and laughed alongside everyone else.

I asked Judy, "what's that thing on the ground? Why is everyone so grossed out by it?"

"They're not grossed out – it's not gross. Everyone's just playing with it. You should touch it," Judy said.

When I looked away from Judy, I realized that everyone was staring at us. The thought of someone actually touching the plastic peaked everyone's interest.

"Go ahead and touch it," she prodded again.

"No...no...I don't want to," I said.

"Come on. Go ahead and touch it," Judy said.

"I'll think about it," I said, hoping she would drop it.

On the one hand, I knew that the crowd's attention wasn't good attention, but at least in some way, I was included in the group. I knew Judy wasn't telling the truth and that the piece of rubber on the ground was something dirty, but I played along.

That moment, they confounded me, these kids who always had to do exactly what everyone else did. When one kid in the group had an idea, the rest of them always followed. It had to be a crowd, never just one or two of them but always the whole crowd. They put someone or something underneath their overactive magnifying glass and watched it, criticized it, even decimated it till annihilation. So it was with this piece of rubber on the ground. So it also was with me.

No one else in their group could fathom doing something which would embarrass them in front of everyone else; they were not brave enough. Though I didn't know it at the time, I was the brave one. I knew what it was like to stand alone, and that was probably why they dared me and not anyone else.

What was so horrific about the inanimate piece of rubber that it deserved such attention? I agreed that it looked disgusting, but was anything really "gross" enough to elicit that kind of reaction? The truth of the matter was that, even at a young age, nothing disgusted me so much as a group, mocking and laughing at something with such intense focus.

With all of their attention on me now, they edged me forward? Would it prove to them that I was as disgusting as the piece of rubber on the ground? Could I do it, this unthinkable act?

"Touch it, yeah touch it," the group chanted.

I considered retreating but changed my mind. I walked over and used the tip of my finger to touch the rubber. I didn't melt. I didn't disintegrate. Nothing of the object was left on my finger, and I wiped my hand on the grass nearby to make sure.

"Ewww!" the kids screeched and yelled.

"Ayesha has AIDS!"

The chant continued as we all walked into the building. "Ayesha has AIDS. Stay away from her, she has AIDS."

The taunt about me having AIDS didn't dissipate that afternoon. On the contrary, it went on for months. In response to the ever-present suggestion that I had a life-threatening disease, I actually became sick. Migraines, nausea, and vomiting plagued me in the following months.

When I told my parents about being made fun of and told that I had AIDS, they were upset enough to allow me to stay home until I had no choice but to go back. The difficulties did not ease when I returned to school.

Why was it so hard? All I wanted was to be accepted as I was, but that didn't seem likely to happen. It was a comfort to think that I could trade places with someone who had everything – confidence, good grades, and friends. What if I could be like one of the kids who everyone loved? What if I could be someone like the Robin?

Well, I couldn't ever be exactly like her because she had beautiful blond hair and sapphire-blue eyes, but maybe one day, I could learn to be as confident and self-assured as she was. Always wearing the coolest brand-name sneakers, she seemed more like a celebrity to me than a middle-school student. Though she was well-dressed and always looked perfect, it wasn't just her outward appearance that made her who she was. Her mind wasn't planted in the mud, the muck that we all knew to be middle school. Anyone could see that she didn't think of the here and now – she thought of a far-off future. Domination wasn't the method by which she gained popularity, like so many others did. She didn't have time to tease or taunt. And, even if the circumstances had presented themselves, which they luckily never did, I knew she wouldn't have wanted to join in and make fun of me. Not a prisoner of isolation, lack of understanding, and ostracization, she had the freedom to think about her goals, her style, and most importantly her future. What would freedom like that feel like?

There was something about her, something familiar, and as I looked at her, walking through those hallways, I saw a beautiful reflection of what I could have been, a girl forging ahead towards her future and protected by all the love and understanding the world could offer. If my family had stayed in Pakistan, I could have been like her, an admired and self-assured girl of the upper class, but the situation here was different – my family struggled for survival. In America, even if I tried my best, I might never be comfortable like her; yes, it would be improbable because others might never understand me. But amidst all the teasing in middle school, I found someone to look up to, someone I could aspire to be more like.

I wanted to show the world that I was, in some way, cool like Robin. I wanted stylish sneakers too, but how would I be able to afford them? Though a child, I still knew that my parents were struggling to establish themselves financially. Forty dollars, the cost of average brand-name sneakers, would be unnecessary spending for our family. Asking them for that kind of money was selfish, so I decided to put the idea out of my head. In fact, I completely forgot about the sneakers until the weekend when I went to the mall with my mother.

When my family lived in Conshohocken, my mom and I spent time in Plymouth Meeting Mall. It was one of the only relaxations my mother had – usually, she spent her time worrying about the family or longing for her old life in Pakistan. On the day in question, the mall was busy. Shoppers ran in and out of stores, but my mother and I strolled slowly. We walked past the food court, and since we were enjoying ourselves already, we treated ourselves to ice cream. I worked on the sweet vanilla cream as it dripped down to the bottom of the cone.

After finishing our ice cream, we headed towards one of the department stores. Walking around in the store, I suddenly halted near the shoe section and noticed a pair of grey sneakers with the green Nike logo on the side. I ran from the aisle of the store into the shoe section. My mother saw me run and followed. For a moment, I'd totally forgotten that she was even in the store. I looked at the price tag. They were thirty-five dollars. Those sneakers were less expensive than so many of the other shoes in the store, yet I knew that thirty-five dollars was still a lot of money. Even though I wanted to, I couldn't ask my mother to buy them because I didn't want to put her into the dilemma of having to buy something unnecessary. I put down the shoes and turned around. *Ammi* stood right in front of me.

"Let me see those shoes," my mother said.

"It's fine. They reminded me of shoes I've seen in school," I said.

"Do you want them?" *Ammi* asked me.

"They're nice, but I was just looking at them. They're too expensive," I said.

"It's okay – you need a new pair of shoes," she said.

"But they're expensive. Are you sure?" I asked.

"Yes, its ok," *Ammi* said.

"Really? If you buy these, I'm not going to ask for anything else for a long time," I said.

Why had she been so casual about spending thirty-five dollars? My father and mother had stopped spending money on themselves – they never bought clothing or shoes that weren't cheap or on sale. Why didn't she expect the same sacrifice from me? There was something wrong with agreeing to let her buy the shoes, but I did so greedily. My parents struggled to make it in a new country, and I let my mother buy me something she would never buy for herself. Who else, besides a parent, would ever do something like that?

My mom paid for the shoes, and I held them in my hands. I stopped considering whether the purchase was right or wrong – those shoes were awesome, and that's all my twelve-year-old brain could care about. Later on as an adult, I realized that the idea that wearing a brand name made you, in any way, a better person was ludicrous, but in middle school, your clothing and shoes meant everything. Back then, I thought I'd walk into school, wearing my Nikes, and the other kids would finally understand that I belonged.

I don't remember exactly what happened the following day, but my new shoes obviously didn't open the doors of popularity for me. It's funny what we do and don't remember. My memories of being left out, teased, or even bullied will never be completely erased from my brain, but I know that my mind tries to minimize remembering them – as the years go by, it tries to crowd itself with whatever was good and decrease the importance of what was bad or ugly. It is decades later, and some memories have been completely ravaged by time – the memories that remain overshadow all that is now meaningless, and in general, the things that are worth keeping tend to stay forever because they're no longer confined to the borders of the mind but are imprinted on the soul.

I will always remember that as a little girl, despite all the teasing, I saw the beauty in others and that it made me happy to know that there were children around me, who could be brave, intelligent, and inspiring. No matter how lonely my life was then, I hoped that one day, the world would see that I could also inspire.

And I'll always remember those shoes because I remember what my parents went through, just to make sure I had the simple things. I have many memories of my mom and dad, a man and a woman who left their homeland to start a new life, and in so doing lost hopes and luxuries that they would never regain. I remember that they, too, were misunderstood by this new place, but that they tried their best, and when they could, they would catch happiness, whether it was in the form of clothing or toys, and willingly hand it over to us, without thinking about what they might want for themselves. Yes, this is a beauty that sometimes crowds my mind, just like it has for so many before me and just like it will continue to do so for so many yet to come.

Chapter 9
Lost and Found
❋ ❋ ❋ ❋ ❋

The fragrance and feeling of fall touched my face, and my first summer away from college ended as quickly as it began. It had turned out to be a very intense and demanding season, but my sacrifices paid off. Managing to save up nearly two-thousand dollars, I'd gathered enough money to be able to pay off my account balance and return for the fall semester.

A few days before the start of classes, I took the hour-long bus ride to Chestnut Hill College. Free from work, I let my mind wander. What would this day bring, would I run into someone on campus, what would I learn in the academic year, and what kinds of students would be in my classes? The more I thought about school, the more I wanted to make sure that everything went smoothly that day. I peered into my bag, making sure that my check book was safe. At this critical juncture, misplacing important items would be disastrous. Besides, obsessively making sure that money, credit cards, and check books were secure had become a compulsive habit.

Today, I'd hand over all the money I'd earned to pay for school. I considered how easy it was to write out a check, but that the struggle of saving two-thousand dollars from a six-dollar-an-hour job would be void from the face of the check. Though my money would soon disappear, the experiences I had in making it were permanently wedged into my consciousness. Since the end of last semester, everything had changed. I'd once thought of those who decided against going to college as simpletons, but I could now understand the decision to delay or even avoid college altogether. The previous year, I'd convinced myself that I'd graduate college and go onto achieve something meaningful and memorable. After that summer though, I doubted whether I'd be able to finish paying for an undergraduate education.

That day, at the end of the summer of 1998, I didn't yet want to hand over the contents of my bank account. To avoid the inevitable financial transaction of the day, I walked around the college. Students had not yet returned and the sights and sounds on the campus stayed subdued.

I went into the cafeteria and bought a plain slice of pizza and a cup of coffee. Pouring the hot liquid into a white, glass cup, I watched the steam float upwards while a distinct, enlivening aroma filled my nostrils. Sitting down with my lunch, I scanned the room. The cafeteria staff ran back and forth, preparing for the next meal. A shared sense of humor spread through the room, making everyone laugh. In between bouts of strenuous activity, an employee would tell a joke. Everybody in earshot would laugh and, after a few moments, would continue with their work. Bouts of joking, laughing, and work continued in a cycle.

After finishing my meal, I walked across campus to Logue Library to visit Gail, who had been my work-study supervisor the previous year. Everyone in the library, including Gail, had become friends with me. As someone who had more life experience than me, Gail used her knowledge to guide me when she could.

When I entered the library, Gail was sitting at the front desk, busy with paperwork, so I greeted her to grab her attention.

"Hi Gail," I said, waving and smiling.

"Oh Ayesha! You're earlier than you said you'd be. How is everything going?" she asked.

I stepped behind the front desk, so I could talk to Gail, face to face.

"I've just been working. Haven't been able to do anything else, really. Just want to come back to school as soon as possible," I said.

"That sounds like when I was in college. Millersville was fun, and I always wanted to go back after break. It was a tough time; your early twenties can be difficult," she said.

"Yeah, my entire summer was about making money. Now I have to deal with all this financial stuff. I could hardly read anything all summer," I said.

"So you haven't even read any of Amy Tan's other books yet?" Gail asked.

"No, I haven't, and I'm surprised I haven't; I thought I'd read all her books right after reading *The Kitchen God's Wife* last year," I said.

"Now that school is starting, you'll have a lot more time to read," Gail said.

"I can't wait to talk more when I'm back on campus, but right now, I guess I should go to the bursar's office and make this payment. I'll see you next week," I said.

"Good to see you too. I'll talk to you next week," she said.

Gail's smiled, and in that moment, I felt that things were already better. A feeling of calm began to occupy my usually anxious mind.

I enjoyed the walk from the library back to Saint Joseph's Hall. As I walked, I took time to appreciate the college. The summer house, tennis courts, softball field, and parking lots were located on the lower level, ten feet lower than the rest of the campus. Then there were the main buildings, including Logue Library, Fontbonne, Fournier, and Saint Joseph's Halls. Logue Library and Fontbonne were freestanding buildings while Saint Joseph's and Fournier were two separate halls housed within the same larger building.

Grey stone covered the entire façade of Saint Joseph's and Fournier. Atop the wall lay orange-colored brick shingles. Small orange towers could also be found at roof level. These towers, along with the windows, gave the college the look of a castle.

After I arrived at Saint Joe's, I ran up the stairs to the second floor. The financial aid, bursar, and registrar's offices were all located in the same hallway. I opened the door to the hallway and, for a moment, began admiring the woodwork. The door frames, leading to the hallway in which the three offices were located, were made of solid carved wood, while the doors, themselves, were made of glass. I walked in. Cool air covered me in a wave and made me realize how hot it really was outside the hallway. Two employees rushed past me. I went into the bursar's office and spoke to a young woman behind the counter.

"Hi, how are you? I think I have a balance that I have to pay," I said.

"What's your social security?" she asked, pushing back her dark and curly hair.

I gave her the number and stood waiting for her response. I hoped that extra funds might have miraculously come into my account and that I could keep my money.

My account came up on her screen and she said, "How much do you want to pay today?"

"I'm paying $2000, by check," I said.

I wrote out the check and handed it to her.

"Ok, thank you. Now, you have an eighteen-hundred dollar balance remaining."

My heart sank and then started to race. I didn't expect to have a remaining balance, especially not a big one like eighteen-hundred dollars.

"Are you sure that I owe money? I think my account should be even," I said.

"I'm showing an eighteen-hundred dollar balance. You'll have to see the financial aid office for additional questions," she said.

As I walked out of the office and into the hallway, the air conditioning blew cold against the sweat on my arms, face, and neck. During the next few moments, my mind and body sent me the contradictory messages of delight and dread. The cold felt comforting regardless of the fact that every new thought and realization felt like calamity. My hopeful disposition was now badly dented, yet my skin separated itself from disaster to experience its own pleasure.

I walked into the financial aid office and asked to speak to someone. A middle-aged man walked in. His brown beard had specks of gray and his hair, slightly receding, stood up naturally and formed spikes. He asked me to have a seat. Explaining my confusion about my balance, I hoped that he would be able to help resolve the situation.

"Yes, I do see that you have an eighteen-hundred dollar balance, which you will need to pay before you can start classes," he said.

"I just paid the bursar's office two-thousand dollars, which took me the entire summer to earn. I can't come up with another eighteen hundred. Can you help me? I really don't want to miss any classes," I pleaded.

"Unfortunately, I won't be able to provide any more financial aid. You're already at your limit," he said.

"Couldn't you please do anything? I'm a good student, and I really need to come back to school," I said.

"Can't you ask your parents? I'm sure they would want to help you," he said.

"I don't want to ask them for that kind of money," I said.

"I'm sorry but you're going to have to come up with it if you want to return to classes," he said.

He excused himself, and as I walked out of the office, the heat momentarily interrupted my desperation. I didn't know whether I wanted to scream or cry. Pangs of sadness pulsated under my eyes and my throat. How could this be? How could I have underestimated the costs so drastically? It must have been my fault. I wasn't going to be able to return to college because I'd messed up.

I thought about the work I'd done over the summer and the excitement I felt when I considered returning to school. Images of earlier hope and optimism made me feel foolish. I ran around elated about something that wasn't a given, and who else would act like that except for an idiot?

I knew myself too well and my attitude was too intense for this type of setback. A missed semester of college meant a broken heart and that meant that I might give up on the whole idea of academics, deciding to focus on something else entirely. On the bus ride home, I felt worse. I was leaving the college campus, and who knew when or if I would ever be able to go back. My racing thoughts started to funnel into anger and then became inextricably linked with disgust. Anger was the only emotion that made sense, after what had happened. I was furious at the financial aid officer, my menial job that hadn't paid enough, other college students who had it easy and never had to do any work, my parents who weren't well-off, and the fact that I made stupid mistakes like miscalculating my student account balance. On top of all of that, the world worked against me. I was sure of it now.

I took a deep breath and tried to think of something positive, but what was there? Even if I went back the following semester, I would be behind, and no one would remember me. Fond memories became acidic and, in the midst of this breakdown, I searched for something, anything, to hope for. After all, how could I, or anyone, handle life without hope?

Alternating faces, from the past year, continued to re-appear in my mind's eye. I couldn't hold back tears as I re-called the faces of friends and faculty who, I thought, would inevitably forget me. If anyone ever remembered me, it would be a hazy picture of a girl who'd attended college for a year and then dropped out without explanation.

Among the many memories of faces, one appeared, which calmed me. This face didn't excite my emotions, like all the others, but somehow seemed to steady them. The persona didn't make me think of the past or the future because its presence was firmly planted in the present. She wasn't animated with expression but communicative and in the middle of explaining something. What could she have to explain now? Whenever she described something, it seemed logical, simple, and good. But wasn't the time for explanations over? What could she have to say to me now that she'd no longer be my professor? The financial aid office had clearly told me that there would be no more professors, no more lectures, and no more classes. As I thought about Professor Sharon Browning, I dried my eyes and took a deep breath.

When I focused on her, something inside me that I thought had drowned, gasped and came to the surface. Suddenly a small shred of hope reemerged. But why? It wasn't like Sharon could snap her fingers and fix all my problems, but she'd probably offer me a kind word like she always did. If I couldn't come back to college the following semester, she would probably be the only one who would understand why. She may have been the only one, in the world, who understood how badly I wanted to go to college.

Luckily, I had Sharon's home number, so I called her.

"Hello," Sharon answered.

"Hi Sharon," I said.

"Oh, hi Ayesha. How are you?" she said. I could tell she was smiling as she said it.

"I'm not good, Sharon. Everything's ruined!" I said.

I didn't give her any further explanation and waited for her to respond.

"What do you mean? Are you safe? Are you hurt?" she asked, concerned.

"My college career is over. The financial aid office told me I can't return this semester because they can't offer me any extra financial aid. I already gave them everything I made in the summer," I said.

I waited for her to agree that my life had been ruined. Being twenty, I hadn't lost my teenaged sense of the dramatic.

"I'm so sorry about that, Ayesha. I can understand why you're upset. I have to go to the college tomorrow. We can meet up there and talk to financial aid again to see if they might consider doing anything to improve the situation," she said.

"Wow, really? Are you sure that's okay?" I asked.

"Of course, I'm sure. You're a good student and deserve a chance, Ayesha. Don't underestimate yourself," she said.

Why was this woman so helpful? She had a daughter my age, but it wasn't like I was related to her myself. Maybe it had to do with her astrological sign. After all, Virgos were helpers, and maybe, that's why Sharon always helped me. Sharon helping me calmed my anxiety because, perhaps, the whole world wasn't really working against me.

"Thank you so much Sharon. If you're sure it's okay, then I will meet you at the college tomorrow at eleven," I said.

"Ok, see you then," she said.

I considered my conversation with Sharon. Was it really true? Could there really be a chance that something could be done? As usual, I couldn't help feeling guilty for using someone's goodness to my advantage, but, I felt reassured by the fact that I wouldn't have accepted Sharon's assistance had I been able to do something to help myself.

I took another bus ride to CHC the following day. I waited for Sharon outside the main entrance of the college and saw her car pull up. She parked in front of Fournier Hall. This may have been my last visit to this college. If I couldn't return for the fall semester, at least I could walk around the campus with my favorite professor, one last time.

After arriving at the financial aid office at Saint Joe's, we waited for the officer to speak with us. Uncomfortable, I shifted back and forth in my seat. Though her big brown eyes showed concern, Sharon remained calm. She ran her fingers through her salt and pepper, shoulder-length hair. I thought that the meeting with financial aid would probably end up being an exercise in futility. What could be done that day when nothing could be done the day before?

The same officer finally came in and had the same expressionless look on his face. He sat down in front of us, and although he had already sealed my fate yesterday, I couldn't help expecting that he hadn't told me the worst of it. I began to listen for bad news. Perhaps he would announce that my matriculation status at Chestnut Hill College had been revoked altogether.

"Yes, how can I help you?" he asked.

"I just wanted to try to see if there's anything more I could do to come back to school this semester. My professor is also here to see if she can help in anyway," I said.

"Ayesha is one of my best students, and I'm really hoping that she could be awarded some more financial aid," Sharon said.

"I'm sorry, but as I told Ms. Habib yesterday, she has been given her full award money for this semester," he said.

"I've written a letter on Ayesha's behalf. I'm hoping you could take it into consideration," Sharon said and handed the letter to the officer.

Without expression, he took the letter. We watched as he unfolded and read it. Sharon had mentioned earlier that she had written a letter on my behalf, but I wasn't sure what it contained.

Though it was difficult to tell what he was thinking or feeling, something shifted in the expression of the financial aid officer's face.

"Just give me a few minutes," he said.

He walked to another section of the office.

"Thank you so much for helping me, Sharon," I said.

"Thank you" was all I could say to Sharon, for the rest of my time with her that day.

The officer returned a few minutes later and said,

"I've determined you can apply for an additional loan, which will allow you to return to school this semester. You will have to fill out this paperwork," he said.

"Wait, what do you mean? If I'm approved for this loan I can return to school?" I asked.

"Yes, so please fill out these pages," he said, leaving the room again.

After I quickly filled out the paperwork, I went into the other room and handed the loan application back to the financial aid officer.

"Ok, thanks. You're all set to return this semester," the financial aid officer said to me.

"Really? Thank you so much! That's great news!" I said.

Humbled by the whole experience, I realized that it had somehow all worked out.

Sharon and I walked out of the office, and I gave her a hug.

"Can you believe it? I can actually come back this semester," I said.

"Sometimes, it's helpful to have someone else go with you. I'm glad you won't have to miss any classes this semester. So, I'll see you next week, right?" she asked.

Her last question made me smile.

"I'll be back next week for sure. See you then," I said.

She smiled back at me and asked if I needed anything more because she had to attend another meeting. After I told her I didn't need anything more, she gave me another hug, walked down the stairs, and disappeared out of sight.

Sharon changed everything. After thinking about what just happened, I imagined that Sharon wasn't a professor at all but an angel, placed at the college to help students like me. I had certainly needed her, and she miraculously intervened to change my future in a profound way.

Chapter 10
Change

✴ ✴ ✴ ✴ ✴

So, that was the day I found out that I'd be able to proceed towards my sophomore year of college. I could no longer afford to live in the dorms, but was beyond thankful for the chance to return to classes. Things were different, but I wouldn't let them change too much.

If only I could have realized that everything had already changed, then I would have saved myself from unnecessary disappointment. Because whether it's longed for or dreaded, everything does change. No matter how much I fought it, change forced me to acknowledge its supremacy over my life.

Freshman year, I loved living in the dorms, but sophomore year, I hated the long commute to campus – riding the bus, to and from college every day, drained me. As a commuter, I no longer knew if I still belonged with the other students. I missed out on college life because I only stayed on campus for a set number of hours while residents lived on campus twenty-four seven. A lot of residents weren't interested in being friends with students who lived off-campus because commuters were, according to residents, strange. No one announced this fact on a loudspeaker, but every time I overheard a group of students gossiping about how strange someone was, without fail, that person would be a commuter. Why were we strange? We were constantly carrying our things around with us, kept unusual schedules, coming and going at odd hours, and spoke of mundane things like our commutes. Naturally, I started gravitating towards other commuters for friendship, which was necessary because my friends from the previous year scattered and formed new clicks, none of which I was a part of – some hung out with the jocks while others started spending all their time with party girls.

My best friend, Molly, started spending more time with friends she'd made freshman year. These friends struck me as trouble from the start. They offered Molly access to things I considered dangerous, things like drugs, parties, and men, things that I didn't want to be around; yes, Molly's new friends peddled a trifecta of danger. Trying to warn Molly about trouble on the horizon made me realize why my parents kept obsessing about the dangers that might potentially confront me.

Why did Molly like these girls so much, anyway? They seemed like morons to me, pissing away mommy and daddy's money on alcohol and marijuana. Why did they stay in college? Why not just rent an apartment and drug the day away? Every time Molly and I went to their room freshman year, they were high. And yes, I was jealous. To have to worry so little is a luxury not afforded to everyone, and it certainly wasn't a luxury afforded to me.

"I hung out with Courtney and Kelly last Friday. I met their boyfriends, and they're really cool. You should give them a chance. You'd like them, I bet," Molly said.

Her statement struck a chord. It was funny that I had to give her new friends a chance. Why did I have to give *them* a chance? As an outsider, what power did I have in the situation?

By this point in my life, being able to sense unease in others had become an asset, and I could tell that her friends were not comfortable around me like they were around her. For some reason, Molly thought it would be simple for me to become friends with her friends. She neither asked her new friends if they wanted to be friends with me, nor did she ask me.

And why did she always think everything as easy as the snap of a finger? How could she ask me to hang out with these women's boyfriends, men who I didn't even know? I might have argued with my parents, but I trusted their views on the subject of men, much more than I trusted anyone else's. The years of lectures, warnings, and punishments for crossing boundaries couldn't be so easily disregarded. Going to coed college parties may have been expected of Molly, but it remained a transgression for me.

Yes, her new friends walked and talked more like her than I did, and they had equally adventurous spirits. In every way, they mirrored Molly with one important exception – Molly was exceptionally studious. Books made Molly as happy as they made me.

For this reason, among others, I didn't want to give up on her friendship. Molly had a way of making you feel important, of making you feel that you were the center of everything. Most importantly, she had a way of making you think that you belonged, with her, her family, and even with the whole world, but the belonging she offered, like anything else in life, was temporary.

Where conversations with Molly were once so interesting, they now started to be superficial. Molly and I headed down a predictable path, a path of divergence. Our differences started to separate us.

I didn't yet want to face the inevitability of what often happens when we grow older. People will befriend anyone when they're young, but as they grow up, they gravitate towards people who are more like themselves in their backgrounds, goals, and tastes. In real life, sameness, not opposition, is what draws us to others.

And no matter what I did or said, it was too late because our arguments had taken their toll. I no longer had the title of best friend, the one to watch out for or make concessions for. The pendulum in Molly's mind had already swung away from our friendship. She had challenged me, changed me, and amazed me with her acceptance, but it no longer mattered to her.

Sadness overwhelmed me because of the drastic changes taking place around me, but there was only so much of it my mind took before it converted everything into anger. When I saw Molly on campus, I ignored her completely. She was like everyone else, like the rest of the world that never understood. I had expected too much from her, but then I expected the worst. I couldn't take any more of that kind of rejection, and there was no going back to that friendship. I'd allowed myself to trust someone without question and learned my lesson never to do it again.

Nevertheless, it happened the way it was supposed to – that friendship needed to end, maybe even the way it did. Instead of standing on my own and using the first year of college to try to figure out who I was, I leaned too heavily on Molly. She fit in so well, so instead of standing fully in the light, I stayed safe in her shadow, but doing so meant burdening her and sacrificing my own power. It wouldn't be the last time, in my life, that I chose the safety of someone else's shadow though I longed for the freedom to stand alone, without any fear.

In addition to Molly, I also lost all of the friends we had in common, so I guess they'd never really been my friends after all. Their joint decision to stop spending time with me put me in a familiar place, the space where I didn't belong anywhere or with anyone. I was officially an outsider, again. And, yes, that was what I'd always be – an outsider in my home and among my relatives where I was too Americanized and a misfit among my peers where I wasn't normal.

I threw thoughts and memories of Molly, and other freshman-year friends I subsequently lost into a specific part of my mind – the part that was quiet, dark, and disconnected from everything around it; though it was isolated, I never underestimated the strength of that still portion of brain matter. Inert as it was, it tried a few times to overwhelm everything else. Yet in times of great sadness, I secretly longed for its dominance, so it could subdue everything else once and for all. It could make everything as still, dark, and quiet as it was. It could help me find an end among its nothingness.

No matter what our feelings may be, anyone who struggles for their goals or tries to make meaning out of their life is an achiever, regardless of what they gain or lose on their journey and what others think about them. And isn't it in our ability to hope and dream that we reach the heights, in our minds and sometimes even in reality. All human hopes and dreams are sacrosanct and are expressions of the limitless human soul.

I had certainly hoped and dreamed of many things, and although there was no material gain, my time at college met a mark. By sitting in the college library, analyzing books, and making connections that forever changed the way I viewed the world, I succeeded. I educated myself in a private American college with a lack of ready financial means because I worked, lived with my parents, and received scholarships for academic achievement.

And regardless of all the anxiety, stress, and confusion, I did complete college on time, graduating with departmental honors in both my majors, French and sociology. I also received a variety of awards for academic achievement. It was a time of acclaim, not just for me, but also for my classmates who had also struggled during their years in college.

Sasha was one of the students who didn't have it easy, but you wouldn't be able to tell by looking at her. In fact, it could be said that she was the most well-dressed and attractive woman at school. Sasha's shoulder-length, brown hair had natural-blond highlights. Her face was heart-shaped with high cheekbones, a wide forehead, and a shapely chin. She had hazel eyes with flecks of a multitude of colors, including orange, green, gold, and brown.

It wasn't just her looks that made her beautiful. She had a poise, charm, and intensity to her that remained a source of interest to some and a source of instigation to others, and although the rest of her was polite, gracious, and feminine, her eyes conveyed an unapologetic intensity that could unnerve. Above everything else, she was brilliant, mastering her majors of French and history with great acumen. So, I went from losing a lot of my friends to having the brightest student on campus become my best friend, and yes, I liked the safety of being in her shadow, but Sasha knew how to gently push me away and into the light so that I could learn to stand bravely by myself.

Sasha helped lift me out of my loneliness. Just like me, she'd gone from living on campus to becoming a commuter, so we both didn't fully belong with the residents anymore – this fact gelled our friendship. Sasha also knew what it was like to feel out of place – her mother's side of the family was Russian, and her maternal grandparents were Holocaust survivors. They made it to America, but never escaped the horror of what they had lived through. After being in America for some time, both Sasha's grandmother and grandfather committed suicide, choosing to hang themselves together on the same day.

So, Sasha's mother had to deal with the loss of both parents and chose to deal with the trauma by developing a lifetime addiction to alcohol. Regardless of her own struggles, Sasha's mother raised her own children with what she saw as discipline. Sasha was raised with a particularly stern, Russian upbringing, which was disproportionately hard on female children. Even as a small child, if Sasha reached over the table to grab something, she was smacked hard by her mother's spoon.

I liked the fact that Sasha felt comfortable confiding in me, and we supported each other so much that, by senior year, we'd become like sisters. We both studied extremely hard and worked a lot of hours outside of school, but I had the opportunity to spend a lot of time with her in classes since we both majored in French.

For me, and perhaps for Sasha as well, eating meals off campus was one of the best parts of the week. Before classes began or after classes ended for the day, we'd head out to the local Manhattan Bagel, and once in a while somewhere else, to buy coffee and a sandwich or bagel. Sasha would usually drive us back and forth and decided what time we returned to campus. She drove quickly and methodically almost as if she were a race car driver in training. We'd walk into whatever café we'd chosen and sit for an hour, or even two, and talk about *everything* while having our meal. One afternoon we sat at Manhattan Bagel sipping coffee and trying to unwind.

"When my mother was alive, she told me exactly how to live. She wanted me to dress well, speak well, and have manners. That's why these girls who come to class in their pajamas drive me crazy," Sasha said.

"Well, you certainly lived up to your mother's expectations, and I don't know what to say about the girls who come to class in their pajamas. It is class after all. I don't think they realize that some people would give anything to be in their place, but they take it for granted. Education is a gift," I said.

"That's why I like you. We always see eye to eye. Don't ever think I've had it easy, Ayesha. Appearances can be deceiving. I'm put together, but I'm nothing like any of those spoiled girls, who don't do their homework and waste their lives," she said.

"Yeah, but it only hurts them to be that way. Think about it. At this point, you can go through Hugo, Balzac, or even Proust like it's no big deal because you put in the work," I said.

"I didn't buy these clothes at the store, Ayesha. Everything I'm wearing is from the thrift store," she said.

"Oh…Your clothes always look so nice though," I said.

"They look nice because I keep them that way, but I didn't go to one of those expensive stores and spend mommy and daddy's money. My mother is dead, and my father doesn't give a damn about me. He's always cared more about his girlfriends than his children. When I was growing up, both my parents were alcoholics. They divorced, and then my mother started bringing home drunk boyfriends," she said.

"I'm so sorry," I said.

"Don't be sorry. They made their choices, but being the eldest child, I ended up raising their kids for them. That's pathetic," she said and waved her hand in front of her in a dismissive gesture.

"If I could have done anything to help you, or if I could have had any effect on the past, I would have done something to make the situation better." I said.

"You're a good person, Ayesha. You're going to have to be careful in the world," she said with a concerned look on her face.

"What do you mean?" I asked.

"Well, people take advantage of people who see the good instead of the bad. You're an idealist, so you have to be careful," she explained.

"I will," I said.

"It's okay. Be yourself, but just be cautious," she said.

Switching the topic, I asked, "I have two major papers to write, and I have to take eighteen credits next semester. Do you think I'll be okay with graduating this year?"

"You'll be okay. Just stay more consistent with your work. You go through these bouts where you are really, really productive, and then you stop all of a sudden. If you plan to continue in academia you'll have to be more methodical with things. This year will require you to plan everything out," she said.

When she spoke on academic subjects, I could listen to Sasha for hours. She was a natural-born teacher. We didn't just discuss academics, and she'd happily give me advice on a variety of topics.

"You don't pay attention, sometimes. Be in the moment, Ayesha. Don't daydream. Stay focused on the task at hand," she lectured.

No matter what her advice, I wasn't offended because I knew that she was just as sincere with me as I was with her. Even when she changed the topic and talked about my clothing, I still listened with an open mind.

"You wear your clothing too big. Your clothes are hanging off you. How are you going to find a job if you're not dressed up?"

"Thanks for your advice Sasha, but I need to be comfortable. I can't have everything tight all the time," I said pulling at my pants to demonstrate discomfort.

"Okay, but if you ever want to go shopping to find things that might be a bit closer to your size, then just let me know," she said.

"I might take you up on that. Maybe you can help me find something that's comfortable as well as professional," I said.

She smiled and said, "Yeah, that's a good idea."

Genuinely caring for my welfare, she wasn't just a friend but also an ally. For a few years in my life, another person seemed to completely understand and accept the person I was, and this was no common occurrence. With Sasha's support and influence, I achieved a level of academic success that I may not have otherwise.

But everything, no matter how perfect it may once have been, always changes. It all started when Sasha asked me to be a bridesmaid at her wedding, which was set to take place right after graduation. Having met her fiancé junior year, she was excited to be marrying him soon.

One day, Sasha and I sat studying in the Irish room at Logue Library. I went back and forth through material I'd collected for my French thesis on Marcel Proust. Similarly, Sasha went through books on the author she was analyzing for her thesis. Wooden book cases with intricate carvings surrounded us. Our things were spread out easily over a huge wooden table, which had the same carvings as the shelves. The entire room was green, including the walls and the carpet.

"Do you want to be in my wedding? You're my best friend. I hope you will," she said.

"Yes, of course I'll do it. What do I need to do?" I asked.

Her upcoming wedding secretly scared me. What would I do without her if she no longer had time for me? When a woman married, she usually didn't have time for her friends anymore, or so I thought. Even if she wanted to talk to me after her marriage, what would we talk about? She would be a mature and fully experienced woman while I wouldn't have so much as kissed anyone yet.

Sasha went on, "Basically, you would support me with wedding stuff and stand in a special area during the wedding itself. You'll have to pay for the dress that I pick out for the bridesmaids."

"I don't do dresses," I said half-jokingly.

"Don't worry. I'll definitely choose something you can wear. It won't be anything too revealing," she said.

"Oh okay. That sounds good," I said.

Later that week, Sasha emailed me with the dress she'd picked out. Though it was modest, it still ended a few inches above the ankle. What was more of an issue though was the v-shaped neckline and the fact that the dress was sleeveless. I called Sasha and told her what I thought.

"The dress is still a bit too much. My parents won't like me to wear it," I said.

"Do you think the dress is trashy?" she asked.

"Well, no, it's not trashy," I said.

"Okay, well stand up for yourself. The dress I've picked out is very classy. I wouldn't make you wear something trampy, Ayesha. Do I ever wear anything trashy? Then why would I make my friends wear something that was?" she asked.

"Yeah, you're right," I said.

I didn't want to argue with her, but I also knew that I ultimately wouldn't be able to do it. I didn't know how to explain to Sasha that the dress wouldn't work, and I didn't want to sneak off like some kind of rebel, wearing it behind my parent's backs. Regardless of what Sasha said, the dress remained unacceptable. In the type of culture my parents came from, it was okay for a woman to wear half-sleeves and even shorter sleeves, but something sleeveless wouldn't do and neither would a dress that didn't come down to the ankle. Instead of confronting her and being clear, I ignored the issue. Weeks went by, and the other bridesmaids had already ordered their dresses.

During the last weeks of college, Sasha's wedding wasn't something I could think about, and I should have declined her request up front. I had six classes to prepare for and worked on my second thesis, which needed to be written and presented entirely in French.

While working on a paper in the library one day, I received an email from Sasha.

"Why haven't you bought the dress yet, Ayesha? My wedding is a few weeks away," she wrote.

I e-mailed back, "I didn't realize it was so soon. I'm sorry Sasha, I'm not sure I can buy the dress. Its seventy-five dollars, and I really don't have the money. Plus my parents aren't going to let me wear it," I said.

She emailed back within a few seconds, "I can't believe you! I thought you were my friend. This is my wedding and will only happen once. I just have to face the fact that you don't care about me," she wrote.

"That's not true. It's not that easy for me to do this. I care about you a lot, but my parents won't like me wearing that dress. You are my best friend. Why do you care so much about the dress? Can't I just come to your wedding without being in it?" I asked.

"I really can't believe you. I've always supported you. I ask you for one thing, and this is what happens. We're done, Ayesha. Don't bother coming to my wedding at all," she wrote.

The emails that were flying back and forth suddenly stopped. I sent a few emails in the following days, but to no avail. I didn't hear from her, and maybe, it was for the best. Maybe I had just hastened the inevitable, the dissolution of our wonderful friendship to reality, but I still had hope. Sasha would be forced into the same room as me when we presented our respective theses to the French Department, but when that day arrived, she sat in the lecture hall, avoiding eye contact with me at all cost. Regardless of everything that had happened, I still expected to talk to her after the presentations were over. It was our routine. After the presentations ended, we spoke to faculty members about our presentations. As I was busy talking, Sasha walked out with classmates, and I didn't see her again till graduation. Even on graduation day, Sasha still wouldn't make eye contact with me. All of this over a dress! If I didn't like dresses before, I really hated them now.

For Sasha it wasn't just about a dress. It was about sharing the most important day of her life with one of her best friends. My friendship with Sasha always reminded me of something wonderful – people can disregard race, religion, and culture, or forget about them completely, coming together because of deeper human truths, becoming blind to the arbitrary things at the surface, and find in others, so different than themselves, understanding, support, and love. Sasha couldn't have been closer to me if she was my sister, but we both let something petty, like a choice in dresses, divide us. I could have just worn that dress and put a shawl over my shoulders, or she could have changed her dress choice, finding something that had a higher neckline. I could have been less selfish and realized that this was her wedding, so it wasn't about me. Instead, just like so many others, we preferred being right over everything else. Countless other conflicts started that way, and now, we had our own to add to the mix.

Later on, I realized that there was something more to my reluctance in participating in Sasha's wedding and a reason I unconsciously drew a line in the sand. It was my way of saying that our friendship was more important to me than anything else, even a wedding. Husbands were important but so were best friends. It wasn't realistic to expect anyone to put her soon-to-be spouse on the same level as her best friend, but by not agreeing to do whatever she wanted for the wedding, like sneaking around and wearing that dress, I expressed the wish to be on par with anyone else in her life. If I really was as important as she said, then she should have changed the rules. She should have let me wear something else. And yes, I was selfish about Sasha's wedding, but the importance she placed on her fiancé had been nudging at one of my pet peeves.

Growing up as the only sister among three brothers, I hated feeling like I was being told to fade into the background and unquestioningly put the needs and preferences of males above my own. I wasn't being logical, but Sasha telling me to wear that dress, or else, reminded me of my mother telling me to let my brothers do something that was at odds with what I wanted. If I was relaxing and watching television after school, I hated being told to stop in the middle of a show and let my brothers decide what they wanted to watch. Sasha putting pressure on me about her wedding, a ceremony to solidify her connection to a man, irritated me in the same way. To my annoyed ears, Sasha was saying,

"Who cares if you find yourself in trouble? You're just a woman, so your life only means so much. I'm talking about my wedding here. This is about my marriage to a wonderful man. Do I care if you don't want to do it? Put on the damn dress."

In my home, it seemed like my brothers were handed things that I had to fight for endlessly. While I longed for a driver's license and simple transportation to and from school, my older brother, Nasir, already had free reign of what was once the family car. Arguing with my parents, I asked why the car automatically went to Nasir.

"How come the rules are different from person to person? Why does Nasir automatically get the car? Do you know how difficult my life is without being able to drive? Why couldn't the car belong to everyone?" I asked.

"Well you can think about buying a car once you have a license," my dad said.

"How am I supposed to have a license if I don't have a car to practice on?" I asked.

"You can practice on my car when I have free time," he said.

"Practicing on your car doesn't help. A small car, like the one Nasir was just handed, would have been helpful, but now that it's been dubbed "his car," no one will ever be able to use it for anything," I said.

In my sophomore year of college, after all the struggle of trying to find someone who would teach me how drive properly, one of my friends, Julie, finally did teach me how. Naturally energetic, Julie seemed to bounce wherever she went. Her high energy level worked to my advantage because she was willing to take on extra projects, like helping me with my driving situation.

On nights when I wasn't scheduled for work, Julie drove us off-campus, so I could practice driving. We would buy dinner and, then, drive to a parking lot where she would let me use her car to practice driving and parallel parking.

"Are you sure it's okay with you that I'm using your car?" I asked Julie.

"Yeah, of course," she said.

"I don't know how to thank you enough. You don't know how hard it's been not being able to drive," I said.

"I can imagine. Don't feel guilty. I'm your friend, and friends help each other," she said.

After a few driving lessons, Julie let me use her small Ford Tempo to take the driver's license test, and using her car, I passed the test the first time – it finally felt like a burden I'd been carrying around had suddenly been lifted. Walking back into the driver's license center, I noticed Julie, seated in a grey, plastic chair. She looked comfortable with her left leg folded over her right one. Her energy couldn't be contained though, and she kept shaking her left leg back and forth. That day, she wore sneakers, like she usually did – it made sense that she always wore sneakers because there was no telling when she would need to sprint somewhere like a class, the store, or the library. On the day of the test, Julie wore a sweat suit. The fact that she was always so casual with her clothing didn't alter the fact that she was fastidious with her school work. As she waited for me to come back from my test, she read a copy of Chaucer's *Canterbury Tales* for the following day's literature class. I walked towards her, so I could share the good news.

Julie looked up and asked, "So, what happened?"

Playfully, I said, "No go. I didn't pass."

"Whhhaaaat? Why, what happened? I thought you would do it this time!" she said.

"Well, I did. When I go over there, they will give me my very own license," I said, pointing towards the line where they gave out driver's licenses.

"Yay! That's awesome!" Julie said and hopped up to give me a hug.

After we let go of each other, we both jumped up and down playfully.

After I passed my driver's test, my dad followed through on his promise of giving me a used car. A white, Ford Taurus station wagon had been sitting idle in our driveway for years. He took it to a mechanic to bring it back to working condition. Being able to drive that car made life much easier.

I wondered why my dad couldn't have just fixed the car earlier and why he let me struggle for years. I know he didn't enjoy watching me suffer. Maybe he thought it necessary to teach me a lesson. When interacting with his kids, he always had a lesson in mind, but I wasn't sure what the lesson had been in regards to my inability to drive. Maybe he wanted to show me that, "Nothing in life is handed to you." Or maybe, my father's unwillingness to help me wasn't unwillingness at all. Maybe he was overwhelmed with his own responsibilities and struggles.

Years after I passed the driver's test, I drove down highway 309 and was filled with feelings of profound gratitude. How strange that I was in the same space I had been, all those years ago, but under totally different circumstances. Back then, I walked towards Montgomeryville Mall, angry and sad that my life had to be so much different than everyone else's. But things had changed. I had the freedom to drive wherever I wanted so long as I could afford the gas, and I was slowly coming to realize that I really didn't want to be like everyone else.

In that moment, I wished that I could reach out to my younger self to talk to her. I wondered what words I would use, if it was possible to pull up to her, walking on the side of the road. Would I commend her on her perseverance and drive on? Would I ask her if she wanted a ride, or would I tell her that the annoying and potentially dangerous walk to work wasn't such a bad thing because the experience was building her character?

Although we might want to, none of us will ever be able to talk to a younger version of ourselves. The only thing that ever comes close to this convenience is following intuition – it was intuition that forced me to repeatedly brave highway 309 years ago. The memory of that desperate girl, running to work or the bus to make her way to college, is the reason that my heart still warms when I see someone, on a street or highway, walking to wherever he or she has to go. My experience is the reason that I sometimes stop to give others rides because this simple act may help someone move closer to a dream.

Chapter 11
Fate

There wasn't anything glorious waiting for me after I finished undergrad, and no one cared about how many academic awards I'd won. When I stopped rushing everywhere, I had more time to myself to think – it was then that I realized that I couldn't really feel anything fully. Joy, love, and want were dull, and the only emotions I experienced to their fullest were anger and sadness. While in college, I'd been so focused on trying to graduate that I hadn't had time to deal with my emotions. At that time, I came to the realization that although I craved love and understanding, it wouldn't be easy for me to find either. And with the completion of college, it felt like I returned to the place I was before I found the potential and promise that academics offered. Having once read handfuls of books a week, I no longer read at all. Although I didn't want to lose the languages I'd learned, French and Russian, I lost more words every day that went by. During school, I'd filled my head with literature and science and hadn't had time to think about the feelings of worthlessness that plagued me, but with school now behind me, the feelings surfaced like a specter and haunted me again. Hope halted and dreams diminished with every day that went by.

Was I really back to where I was before I found academics? Was I really back to being that child who foolishly planned to kill herself? By the time I was twelve, suicide became a regular consideration, but the only time I considered carrying out an attempt was when I planned on swallowing an earring to end all my suffering. I thought about the internal damage such an act would cause and wondered whether it would be enough to facilitate an exit from the world.

One day after school, I sat in my bedroom, while my mother and brothers watched television in the living room. I leaned on my bed, staring at the design on top of my blanket – two cartoon elephants with their trunks linked together and big red hearts floating above their elephantine heads. Magazine pictures were taped to the room's walls along with some of my own drawings, like one of a colorful cartoon girl with ponytails jutting out from the side of her head.

My mind became focused on attaining peace by ending it all. Unscrewing the artificial earring from my right ear, I felt its sharpness in my hand. I moved the earring in front of me, put it in my mouth, and held it there. This was the right thing to do. I didn't belong anywhere or with anyone. That is how it would always be, and I would be bullied my whole life. I braced myself to swallow but started crying instead because I couldn't do it. After a few moments, I took the earring out of my mouth. I cried for the rest of that afternoon, and after that day, the idea of suicide surfaced again, but I never made another plan to carry out an attempt.

That was years ago, but would my life return to that dark place? With academia behind me and the lack of any positive changes in my life, I became despondent, hopeless, and lazy. I'd wanted to continue my education at the master's level, but it wasn't in the cards. My ambition, drive, and focus all but vanished, but maybe at the time, losing all my motivation was what I needed. Worrying about my education had given me enough anxiety and stress to last me a lifetime, and trying to become successful had taken a toll on me. I no longer feared being left behind because I was already there. At this point, I didn't have anything to lose, so I let myself go. For the time being, I didn't want to worry about anything. Instead of trying to find a better job, I continued working at the same place I'd worked for the past three years, a marketing research firm called Butler and Associates.

Often, I went out with my work friends after the shift ended and sometimes stayed out later than my strict ten o'clock curfew allowed. The curfew seemed unfair to me, but what could I do about it? I felt that I didn't have the know-how to move out, and aside from my parents, I didn't really have anyone who could help me in a time of need. Family was family, and friends were friends. Friendships, although they could make you feel like a part of something, only went so far. Even if I could manage to move out, I didn't want to alienate my parents by doing so.

But after years of working at Butler and Associates after college, I finally left. I started to work at a new job as a customer service representative for a pharmaceutical company, but after six months of working at my new job, I became completely bored. There no longer seemed to be anything inspiring left in my life.

By the time I was twenty-five, I was worn out from meeting the expectations of two cultures, the culture of the country I'd come from and the one in America that still remained, at times, confusing. Surely, there must have been something that could change things and give me some stability in my life.

My parents always thought that marriage would help me, and insisted that, someday, I should become a wife because a husband would make me happy and protect me from all the uncertainties and dangers in the world. Maybe marriage really was the answer. Maybe a husband would make me happy, protect me, and stabilize my life. Yes, I'd have all that a woman could wish for, *freedom, understanding,* and *love.* The time had come for me to move out and finally live on *my own terms.*

But, finding a husband would be complicated, and I'd have to come up with an alternate way of doing so besides dating. My parents wouldn't allow me to date, and I wouldn't really have known how to find a date, even if I could. For someone like me, a matrimonial website became the obvious solution. I went onto websites with eligible singles and posted information about myself along with my picture. Eventually, a reasonable response came in – the mother of a man, who lived in Jersey City, New Jersey, called me.

"Hello, is this Ayesha?" she asked.

"Yes, it is. Who is this?" I answered.

"I'm calling about your profile. I wanted to talk to you about some things. Do you have time now….to talk…. about my son….would you like to know more about my son?" she asked.

Looking back on it now, I can still hear her voice and hear in it how much she cared for her son.

"Oh you're calling from the wedding website?" I asked.

"Yes, I want to talk to you about your bio," she said.

"I can talk to you after you call my parents. I need them to talk to you first. Here is their number," I said.

"Okay, thank you. I'll call them," she said.

This was the only way I knew how to approach this kind of phone call. I couldn't just talk to this family in private, and I certainly couldn't set up some sort of secret meeting and fraternize with this woman and her son without my parents being involved. After all, I had no idea who they were. In a worst case scenario, this family could have called with some ulterior motive like murder or mayhem. Whatever my thoughts may have been, this woman, Mrs. Ali, would later tell me that my insistence on involving my parents had impressed her.

A few days later, she followed up with my parents like she said she would, speaking mainly to my mother. Before I went to work one day, my mother said, "A Pakistani woman called about you the other day."

Not knowing exactly what my mother was talking about, I asked, "About what?"

"She told me about her son. He's twenty-eight and lives in Jersey City, New Jersey," my mother said.

"Oh, I think that's close to where Alison lives now," I said.

"Forget about your friends for a second," my mom said.

"What did the woman want?" I asked.

"They want to meet up with you. Maybe, we will be given a *rishta*," my mom said.

"A marriage proposal? But we don't even know them," I said.

"Well, they want to meet us," my mom said.

"Did she tell you anything about her son?" I asked.

"He has a B.A. and works as a journalist," my mom said.

"Why doesn't he have a masters yet?" I asked.

"I don't know. I'm going to keep talking to her and find out more about them," my mom said.

"Okay, whatever. Right now, I'm happy with the way things are. It's fine if they don't call back," I said.

However, the conversations continued. All having been residents of Karachi for a number of years, my parents and potential mother-in-law felt at ease with each other. Though Mrs. Ali and her son lived in the United States, the rest of the family was still in Karachi. After a few phone calls, a meeting was set up so that both families could speak to each other, face to face.

The day before my meeting with the family of this twenty-eight year old journalist, fate intervened. I became stranded in Jersey City, New Jersey, the same city where my potential husband resided but a hundred miles away from my parent's home, the location where the meeting needed to take place. Staying over my best friend's apartment, I'd happily driven us to neighboring Jersey City on Saturday afternoon where we enjoyed dining and shopping at the local mall. Towards late afternoon, I parked my car in front of Pep Boys.

I asked Alison if I should worry about leaving the car in front of Pep Boys all afternoon. She said "I'm not sure." We decided to risk it and leave the car in the Pep Boys parking lot.

I met Alison at one of my customer-service jobs and both being recent college graduates with a similar sense of humor, we hit it off instantly. I noticed her in the office one day, joking with a coworker. Her colorful, hazel eyes and curly, brown hair seemed to match her playful personality.

Strolling into the Jersey City Mall that afternoon, we joked about one thing or the other. She teased anyone and everyone. Knowing that I had a good sense of humor, Alison often directed her jokes at me.

"Please don't trip again. I know you love to tripping all over the place, but don't do it today," she said.

"Oh my God. Do you remember when I fell in front of that Greek restaurant?" I asked.

"How could I forget? Your change went all over the street. I thought you were walking beside me and, all of a sudden, I looked up and noticed that a pregnant woman was holding a bag that looked just like yours. That's when I realized you were on the ground and she was holding your purse." We both giggled.

After a couple of hours of lounging in the mall, we came back to the parking lot to retrieve my car. It turned out that cars weren't supposed to be left in the parking lot after all and that the employees at Pep Boys had my car towed. I immediately called the towing company and waited for someone to answer on the other line. When a man answered, I said,

"Yes, hello, you just towed my car. It's a white, Toyota Echo," I said.

"Yup, I have it here. We're open for another twenty minutes, and we're closed on Sundays. If you can't come here today, you'll have to wait till Monday," he said.

There was no way I'd be able to make it to the tow shop in twenty minutes. I called my parents, who already disliked the fact that I stayed at Alison's apartment on the weekends, to explain the situation. My mom picked up, but immediately handed the phone over to my dad who became instantly irritated. Regardless, I explained the situation to my father, and he said,

"I don't want to hear any stories. You know you have a meeting tomorrow."

"I'm not lying," I said.

"Find a way back here or else," he said.

Regardless of my car being taken, I'd been calm up until that point, but suddenly my stress level skyrocketed.

"What the hell?" I shouted.

He'd already hung up. A combination of anger and fear continued to crowd me.

"What the fuck?" I said to Alison.

"What, they didn't take it so well?" she asked.

"We have to find my car. Do you know where this address is?" I asked.

"I think it's in that direction," Alison pointed.

I explained that we needed to make it to the towing garage fast. We ran for what seemed like a couple of miles. Somehow, we navigated our way to a place we'd never been, passing brick buildings, apartment complexes, stores, and hotels. Although there wasn't an abundance of trees in Jersey City, we flew past a few, embedded into holes in the concrete sidewalks. Trying not to look awkward as we ran, we giggled at the absurdity of the scene. We made it the towing garage just in time and retrieved my car after paying the bill. Although the situation had been irritating as it unfolded, my friend and I later laughed all the way back to her apartment in Hoboken.

Chapter 12
Families

✹ ✹ ✹ ✹ ✹

So, I made it to the meeting the next day. I looked my best, wearing an ornate outfit my mother picked out – it was a black *shalwar-kameez* with colorful patterns and tiny mirrors on orange embroidered cloth on the front of the shirt. I tied the top of my hair in a small pony tail while the rest of it hung below my shoulders.

My family and I waited for the guests to arrive. Following the customary cultural protocol in regards to this type of meeting, I sat in another room when my potential in-laws first arrived. The den was removed enough from the living room so that the guests wouldn't be able to see into it. Staring at the light blue walls and green carpet ahead of me, I wondered why I had to sit in another room. I came to the conclusion that Pakistanis probably saw this rule as another way of keeping unmarried women secure. Asking the potential wife to sit in another room while her family received guests meant that she wouldn't have to interact with strangers new to the home. This enabled her family to weed out unacceptable offers without allowing the potential groom's family to see what she looked like. In considering this reasoning further, I wondered how this could potentially keep a woman safe. I came to the conclusion that if the potential groom's family didn't know what the woman looked like, then they wouldn't ever be able to contact her independently.

I listened from the other room as my family members introduced themselves and spoke to the guests in turn. After a few minutes, my parents called me to join them. Walking into the living room with my entire family and potential in-laws there, I was nervous. Since the day was overcast, the lights in the living room remained on. The living room felt like a stage of sorts. The guests sat in front of the large living room window and accompanying, salmon-colored, vinyl blinds. With guests present, the three, cream-colored sofas were filled to capacity, so that kitchen chairs served as seats for my brothers and cousins. I noticed immediately that the man sitting on the sofa had a handsome face. As I entered the room, both the man and his mother politely acknowledged my presence and then stood up. After I sat down, they followed suit.

My potential husband had a thin frame and was roughly the same height as me. He had curly black hair, big brown eyes, and a sharp nose. He wore black pants and a matching black shirt. During this meeting, I didn't talk much and neither did my potential husband, but I learned that his name was Hamza and that he'd come to the United States when he was eighteen to pursue a bachelor's degree. Having attended Franklin and Marshall College, he'd completed a BA in Economics. He now worked as a journalist for some type of financial magazine in New York City. Hamza's mother, Mrs. Ali, dressed in an understated *shalwar-kameez*. She wore gold bangles, necklaces, earrings, and thick glasses which she adjusted periodically. Although her hair was dyed, probably with *henna*, some grey hair still showed. Mrs. Ali told us about her career as a history professor and that she'd recently had a chance to teach at Franklin and Marshall.

Mrs. Ali's affection for her son became immediately apparent. Instead of calling him Hamza, she lovingly called him "Mr. Hamza."

"Mr. Hamza has made us all proud. When he was eighteen, he came to America, all by himself. He studied hard and graduated from a good school. It's not easy finding a job after you're done, but Mr. Hamza kept at it and found one in New York. Now, he works very hard and stays organized," Mrs. Ali said.

"Looks like you've achieved a lot over the years," my mother said to Hamza.

Hamza smiled and said, "I try."

"He's just being modest. Hamza has accomplished a lot," Mrs. Ali added.

During the meeting, my mother was polite and friendly, whereas my father seemed happy and excited, probably at the prospect of me settling down and starting a family of my own. I could tell that he couldn't see any potential pitfalls to this arrangement. Over the years, I realized that my father was an idealist – he spoke of things the way they should be and not the way they actually were. In his mind, I would be married and live happily ever after, and my marriage would bring me unquestioned safety and security.

My brothers attended this meeting along with my mother's sister, her sons, and her husband. In general, my aunt's family loved to meet new people and socialize, and they carried much of the afternoon's conversations. Both my mother and aunt dressed up, wearing silk outfits and their best jewelry. My father, uncle, brothers, and cousins also dressed nicely, although less formally.

My mother was less reserved than usual and asked Hamza, "So your mother says that you work in New York. How do you like it there?"

"It's great – I love the city," Hamza responded.

"What do you like about it?" she asked.

"No matter what time of day it is, there's always something going on. Also, I've made a lot of friends there, and I really like the place that I work," Hamza said.

"Sounds like fun," my mother responded.

My cousin, Osman, who had attended the same school in Karachi as Hamza, asked, "So, is there any news from grammar school?"

"No, I haven't heard anything, except that Mr. Ahmed left the school. I'm sure the grammarians are carrying on though," Hamza said.

"They always do," my cousin said.

The topic of being a Pakistani ex-patriot came up. Embarrassment welled up in me when I realized that my dad was going to take this opportunity to lecture the whole group about remembering the culture of your homeland.

"We like to keep to our cultural values, even though we're in America. In our home, it has been okay for the children to take part in the good parts of this culture, but the children know that they're not to participate in any of the questionable things like drinking and dating. We've been especially strict with Ayesha," he said.

This was my father's way of talking me up and letting the guests know that I was a "good girl." I never thought I would hear it, but I then received what sounded like an apology. Without looking at me, it seemed as if he was saying sorry to me for being so strict, but why did it take these strangers for him to say these things?

"Ayesha's a dedicated girl. Once she puts her mind to something, she does it. She wanted to go to the college she wanted, when she wanted, and she made it happen. She is a good person and will stand up for others. She will protest things that are wrong and she's actually gone to some anti-war protests," my dad continued.

Hamza smiled and asked me, "So, I take it you're not a fan of Bush?"

I smiled but didn't say anything.

After our group conversation, we had a late lunch. My mother and aunt had prepared a feast, including spiced rice, Chicken Korma, vegetables, bread, and dessert. My parents, aunt and uncle, and Hamza's mother continued conversing with each other near the dining-room table.

I also stood near the table, and Hamza stood next to me, which made me feel awkward but excited at the same time. After a few moments, Hamza did something that, for me, was completely novel. It was something I couldn't remember experiencing before, although I'm sure that male acquaintances might have done similar things. Pouring soda into a clear plastic cup, Hamza handed me a drink before pouring a drink for himself. Even better than the fact that this cute guy gave me attention that evening was the fact that my parents completely ignored our interaction. Hamza and I sat next to each other to finish the meal. Mrs. Ali and Hamza left shortly after lunch.

Before leaving, Hamza looked at me and said, "Bye Ayesha. I'll talk to you soon."

After they left, I told my parents not to become excited because I didn't think they'd actually call us back. Men, especially nice looking ones like Hamza, had never before expressed any serious interest in me.

My father said, "Don't worry. If you like him, just behave the way you did tonight. Don't start any debates, and you'll be fine."

After hearing this suggestion, I decided that if Hamza called me back, then I would stay quiet like I did that night.

I did have a tendency to say too much. The best thing would probably be to let Hamza talk. After all, I liked him. How did I know that I liked him? He was cute. If, on the off chance, he ended up wanting to marry me, I already knew that I would say yes.

To my surprise, Mrs. Ali called us back, and our families continued communicating with each other. If they hadn't called, I would have been disappointed, but it wouldn't have been the worst-case scenario. Hamza rejecting me, after he found out who I really was, would actually be worst.

A month after Mrs. Ali and Hamza visited our house, my parents and I went to Franklin and Marshall College to visit them. Due to the fact that Mrs. Ali taught classes there, she rented the second floor of a house on campus. The drive to meet them ended up being a scenic one as we took winding roads, which passed through rural areas, farms, and open fields. When we arrived, my father parked the car in front of Mrs. Ali's house. We went up to the front door and rang the bell. Holding up the second floor of the house, wooden columns had intricate designs carved into them. White paint covered the porch, the front door, and the shutters covering the windows in the front. The house look clean and inviting.

Mrs. Ali greeted us at the door, and we followed her to the second floor. Again, my parents and Mrs. Ali started chatting. I hadn't forgotten the promise I'd made to myself regarding staying as quiet as possible when I was around my potential in-laws.

Like our party from the previous month, a sizeable meal was served. Today, the meal included small, spicy, beef kebabs, rice mixed with peas, potatoes and peas, *naan* and yogurt sauce. We all ate together and commented, in turn, on how much we liked the food.

"They are just some simple recipes," Mrs. Ali said.

That afternoon, we found out that Hamza currently didn't have a United States citizenship or green card. He had a work visa and needed a green card to stay in the country. This fact made me feel sympathetic towards him, and although I wasn't allowed to open my big mouth, I wanted to say, "Don't worry. If we're hitched soon, you won't have to worry about going back to Pakistan."

I definitely liked the fact that if we married, then Hamza wouldn't have to worry about visas anymore because I had a U.S. citizenship. Even though there wasn't yet any talk of marriage, I already wanted to help this man who had bravely travelled so far and lived alone in New Jersey. Even though I didn't talk much, I liked being in Hamza's presence and looked forward to our next meeting. Following that afternoon, we met up a few more times.

Some months later, our families met again, at my parent's house. The previous night while talking over the phone, Hamza had hinted that he wanted to talk about something important. Again, my aunt and uncle traveled down from Connecticut to be present for the meeting. With both of our families there, Mrs. Ali suggested that Hamza and I become engaged.

"Are you all okay with this idea?" Mrs. Ali asked.

"I'm okay as long as Ayesha is okay," my dad answered.

"It's fine with me," I said.

"After the wedding, you would have to move up to Jersey City, Ayesha. Is that okay with you?" Mrs. Ali asked.

"It won't be a problem to move up there," I said. Of course it wouldn't be a problem, I thought to myself. I would be free to do whatever I wanted. Freedom sounded wonderful.

"This isn't something to jump into. Do you two think you could live together and build a life together?" Mrs. Ali asked.

"Yeah, we've thought this out," Hamza said.

"We're compatible," I agreed.

"Okay good. We don't have a ring today, but, in a few weeks, we could all go to a jewelry store together and pick one out. We will plan out the wedding over the next few months," Mrs. Ali said.

Happiness welled up in me, but a cynical part of my brain didn't allow me to get overly excited because it understood that nothing ever went according to plan. Why did Mrs. Ali ask all those questions about compatibility – did she think we were incompatible?

One night over the phone, Hamza told me that he smoked cigarettes. I thought about what Mrs. Ali had said about compatibility. The fact that Hamza smoked bothered me. A person could smoke when they were young, but who kept smoking after that, even when they were twenty-eight? I decided that after we married, I would help him quit this unhealthy habit.

It turned out that smoking was just one thing, among many, that made us very different from each other. We definitely should have known each other better, and I wish that I had spoken more before we married. I wish he had found out who I really was, a curious woman but not curious about the same things as him, a woman who definitely loved and cared but who was no longer capable of fully feeling or loving things without distance or a pervasive fear of loss, who only experienced sadness and pain to the fullest because they had become the constants, and a woman who could be severely depressed. Nevertheless, I assumed that marrying a man would change or at least alter my state of mind. I'd seen other women grow more positive after they'd settled down, and I figured the same thing would happen to me.

After the engagement, Hamza and I met up independently a couple of times. For our first meeting on a cold day in winter, my parents dropped me off in Center City. Again, I wore traditional Pakistani clothing and a sweater. Regardless of the fact that we were engaged, I still felt insecure around him, waiting for the moment when he discovered that marrying me would be too difficult.

After a few minutes of walking around, he said,

"You're not wearing a coat. You must be really cold."

"Yeah a bit, but I'm okay," I said.

"Let's find a restaurant and stay inside," he said.

"Okay. That sounds good," I said.

We walked into a Chinese restaurant where reds and yellows dominated the walls and tables. The hostess sat us at a table that looked like it was made of cherry wood.

"Seems like an interesting place," he said.

"Yeah, it's nice," I agreed.

"I'm glad we can spend some time together, just you and me," Hamza said with a smile.

"Yeah, me too," I agreed again.

The last thing he said suddenly made me cautious. I didn't trust Hamza because he wasn't yet my husband. Right now, the extent of our relationship consisted of a ring and a promise to marry. The agreement was still subject to change.

Sitting at the table, I remembered the South Asian saying my parents had relayed to me, which stated,

"When an unmarried man and woman are each other's only company, the devil joins them as the third party." The devil wasn't invited to this table though. I wasn't going to throw myself at Hamza, and sex wouldn't be had until we married.

"You're going to like living near New York City. If you like this restaurant, then you'll love Chinatown. There are so many places I have to take you to – Chinatown, the East and West Village, and Brooklyn. Once you move there, I'll have to show you how to move around the city. You'll have to learn which trains go where," Hamza said.

"Yeah definitely," I agreed, still wondering about the Pakistani saying and whether the devil really haunted people as they tried to go about their business.

"It'll be nice when we're both working in the city," he said.

"Yes, it will," I said.

After the meal was done, we walked outside and waited for my dad to pull up. I already knew what time I was supposed to leave and had called him a few minutes earlier to let him know exactly where I was.

"You really should have worn a coat. It's really cold out here," Hamza said.

"I know. I should have," I agreed.

I started to wonder if I had angered Hamza, or if he thought me stupid for not having worn a coat. Maybe, he didn't really care about the coat and criticized my decision not to wear one because he didn't really like me anymore. Maybe, this would be the day that he started to dislike me.

But, he continued to call me, and things moved forward as planned. A few weeks later, Hamza and I met up again. This was the second time we went out unchaperoned. Having planned out what we were going to do, I met Hamza in Chestnut Hill, and we walked around, admiring small stores, which sold colorful arts and crafts. I stayed agreeable and silent, the way I always did around him. After we finished eating dinner in one of the local restaurants, he drove me home. I wouldn't see him again until the wedding.

Though I wanted the week to go well, I remained more stoic than a typical bride. Within a few days, the wedding loomed before me. My parents reserved a large room at the Sheraton King of Prussia where the event would take place. They invited most of the wedding guests, mostly relatives, nevertheless, I wanted to make sure that a few of my professors and friends from Chestnut Hill College also attended.

The day before the wedding was hectic. Relatives, who I hadn't seen for years, started to fly into town – they had all but forgotten that I existed until my wedding. Nonstop activity continued well into the evening before the wedding. Regardless of the variety of tasks I had to do, I still had to keep *henna* on my hands, and I was scared that wearing it would interfere with my sleep before the big day. Although I questioned the necessity of wearing *henna*, I knew I would have to because it was a long-held custom for a South Asian bride to have this mud-like material on her hands before her wedding day.

When the time for sleep finally came, I went into my bedroom and realized that that night would be the last time that I slept in that room, the room that I had grown up in. Exhausted, I changed into my pajamas and, because of the *henna* still heavy on my arms and hands, gently moved into bed. I thought about the significance of the following day, but I didn't necessarily want to think about it. Needing to take my mind off the wedding, I thought of other things and was able to fall asleep right away.

I woke up at ten, took a shower, and finally washed off the *henna* – I was happy to see the dark orange tattoo left in place of where the *henna* had been. The wedding day was as busy as the previous day. My family waited as relative after relative arrived.

One of my father's sisters took on the role of my personal advisor and kept giving me a variety of suggestions. Throughout the day, she told me everything she could about marriage.

"Don't be nervous. You'll be fine. This is a good thing that you're doing. Don't interfere in his family's affairs. Remember that he has an independent relationship with his mother. You should never meddle in their relationship," she said.

By two o'clock, it was already time for me to head to the hotel. My mother, my father's sister, and her daughter went to the hotel while my father and brothers stayed at the house with the guests. Arriving at the hotel with plenty of time left, we went to my room. My parents had arranged for a makeup artist to meet me there, so we all waited for her arrival. That week, I agreed to take part in a lot of primping, that I usually avoided, because I wanted to look nice for my future husband. After all, a woman was supposed to look nice for the man who married her.

The makeup artist arrived a few minutes after me. She first helped me to put on my wedding outfit. Selected by Mrs. Ali and made specifically for me by a tailor in Pakistan, the outfit was a creamy gold color. A large, red border ran along the cream cloth, and heavy, gold ornamentation covered the entire outfit. After helping me navigate the outfit, the artist helped me put on makeup, made my hair, and placed false eyelashes on top of my real ones. Finally, she pinned the heavy shawl, weighed down with ornamentation, onto my hair. When everything was done, I turned around so that everybody could see me. They all looked at me somewhat shocked.

"Oh my God, she looks beautiful," my cousin said.

"She looks great!" my mother said with a combination of joy and sadness on her face.

"It's not too gaudy, is it?" I asked.

"No, it's great," they all agreed.

My mother looked so proud of me, and for a moment, I thought she might cry, but she remained composed. My mother wore a gold-colored *sari* with a border of brighter gold. She also wore makeup and her best jewelry. At times, she seemed to be beaming. Although my dad wasn't too dressed up, he wore a blazer over his pants and shirt. My brothers, on the other hand, wore suits.

Although we'd arrived extremely early, everything that we'd done, up until that point, had taken up a lot of time, so it was almost time for the ceremony to begin. The guests were all waiting. Before we knew it, it was six o'clock. Using an elevator, my mother and I arrived at the first floor where my father met us. We walked down the hall where the wedding would take place.

After my parents and I walked into the room, everyone looked up, and the whole room was quiet – the guests who knew me saw my transformation and looked on with approval. Scanning the room, I found where I had to go. The stage sat at the center of the room. A series of steps led up to two large chairs that had the same shiny gold and silver ribbon that filled the room.

I went up to the tiny, make-shift stage and sat down. As expected of a Pakistani bride in front of so many onlookers, I stayed silent.

After thirty minutes, the *malwee* performed the marriage ceremony, and the room again became silent. The *malwee* recited text from the *Koran*. I looked towards the table where my college friends and professors sat. Alison and her brother Josh sat at the same table. Alison sat composed, but still managed to give me silly looks which made me want to laugh. After the *malwee* finished, both Hamza and I signed marriage contracts.

The guests were now free to eat dinner. Hamza and I stepped down from the stage and sat at a table with my parents, Mrs. Ali, and my mother's sister and her husband. Although marrying Hamza would turn out to be the worst decision I'd ever made made, the looks on my parents' faces still made it one of the best days I'd lived to see. They beamed, and no matter what happened in the following months or years, I'm so glad that I'd given them this – a day of pure happiness and pride, a day when they were admired, just like they had been in their homeland, and a day when sadness and worrying left them. My mother's sister sat next to my parents and looked towards me with tears in her eyes; she cried from joy. Like my father, my aunt thought that I'd finally made it. She thought that my life would be safe and secure from then on. Earlier on, I had seen her intensely mouthing prayers of protection to herself, along with my mother, when the *Koran* was being read.

About an hour after dinner, most of the guests left. Close relatives stayed and continued talking. Our families told us that Hamza and I could leave, so we went back to what was now our hotel room. That night, I took part in what my peers kept telling me I was missing out on all those years – it was significant, but not earth shattering or mind blowing as I had heard it described.

Even though my body experienced human connection over the next few months, it wouldn't allow my heart or mind to follow suit. I was married, but I didn't forget that things never went according to plan. I admired my husband, but couldn't fully trust him, just like I couldn't fully trust anyone.

Chapter 13
Coming Back Full Circle
✺ ✺ ✺ ✺ ✺

After I moved to Jersey City, I worked a few temporary and part-time jobs and had trouble finding permanent work. After some time though, I interviewed at the Middle Eastern Center, a non-profit organization in Brooklyn. Just being invited to an interview for a permanent job was a welcome reprieve. The day of the interview, excitement and nervousness ran through me. That could have been the day I finally attained a job I really wanted, but if the interview didn't go well, I'd have to keep settling for mediocre jobs that didn't require a college education.

I needed this job, and I wanted to make a good first impression. Before heading out, I focused on my appearance. I ran a brush through my hair and adjusted my earrings. I put on a navy-blue pantsuit and made sure that my shoes were polished.

Preparing to head out the door, I put on my coat and grabbed my bag. As I walked out of the apartment building's front door, the cold air hit me. Moving towards the bus stop, I saw the bright reflection of light bouncing off the Hudson River. The vastness of New York City, its skyscrapers, buildings and banners, were visible from the Jersey side of the river. At the end of the street, I waited for one of the little buses that drove into NYC every other minute. As was typical during workdays, a few people were already lined up, also waiting for a bus. Everyone was extremely well-dressed as they always were in that area.

After I arrived in Manhattan, I took the Two Train from Port Authority to Court Street, Brooklyn. Stepping out of the subway, I was struck by the number of buildings overhead. A crowd of people rushing towards work almost ran into me while I stood observing the surrounding architecture. Small shops took up space on the street, and there didn't seem to be anywhere to move.

You name it, and you could find it there – vendors of all sorts were busy with their goods, even during this cold February morning. The smell of spices from the Middle Eastern Gyro Stands permeated the air. Everything seemed to be happening at once. The sights and sounds overwhelmed. I saw what seemed to be people from every part of the world, South Asia, East Asia, Africa, and Europe, interacting with each other. My nervousness dissipated as I walked down Court Street, trying to process all the people and their movements. The scene unfolding in front of me subdued one of my worst fears, to be singled out as strange. I had always been the one who never quite fit in, for one reason or another. From grade school up until that point, so many had taken time to point out this obvious fact. At different points in my life, this fear fomented and I chose to either run from it or face it. Yet, on this cold day on Court Street, my fears lost their power over me because everyone was different, everyone was immigrant, everyone was strange, and everyone was dazed, confused even – I fit in completely because everyone there had also navigated their way through the maddening confusion. Stuck between worlds, we'd all survived our own borderland and ended up in Brooklyn that morning.

I continued walking towards my interview and knew where it would take place because, a few days earlier, I'd made the journey to Brooklyn to familiarize myself with the area. I stepped into a Starbucks across from Middle Eastern Center's office. That Starbucks was a cozy one with couches. Since I had an hour to wait until my interview, I bought and read the *New York Times*.

As I sat there, I thought to myself, "Happiness would be starting out every day as productively as today. If only I'd be given this job, I'd work hard for them all day and then come to this coffee shop, start applying for master's programs, and read to keep my mind sharp."

When it was time, I went into the building and ran up the stairs to the third floor. As I entered the office, I noticed employees moving to a meeting. After speaking with the receptionist, I sat down and waited. Nervousness nudged at me. Looking at the wall in front of me, I noticed its bright coral paint and children's drawings taped to the wall. My mind became focused on one drawing that had a group of children holding hands and playing.

After a minute, the receptionist told me to follow her. I was called into a room in the very back of the office. A petite woman with long brown hair was sitting at a desk, facing away from the door. Large windows covered the office's walls and let in an abundance of natural light and a clear view of the adjoining neighborhood.

As she turned around, I could tell that she was well-dressed, confident, and stunning.

I said, "Wow, you have a great view of Brooklyn!"

"Yes, definitely. I'm Hanan, nice to meet you," she said.

"Very nice to meet you," I responded.

"We called you in to interview for the Case Planner position because your resume had a lot of the skill sets that we look for in candidates for this position. Why did you apply to this job?" she asked.

"I applied because I think I would be great fit. I know that your clients are oftentimes immigrants from the Middle East and South Asia. I can relate to the struggles that these clients may be going through because I've gone through and overcome similar issues. I would like to take my experiences and contribute to lessening the struggles that others are going through."

Hanan asked me other similar questions, and then she talked about Middle Eastern Center and explained that it was a Preventive Services Agency. She went onto explain that the mission of Preventive Services was just that, to "prevent" children from being placed in foster care. I listened intently and answered Hanan's questions to the best of my ability.

After the interview, I took an hour to explore Court Street and then headed down to the subway to start my trip back to New Jersey. When I arrived in Manhattan, my phone rang. Middle Eastern Center was on the other line, and Hanan's assistant asked if I could start work the following week. I stayed calm on the phone and let her know that I'd be more than happy to start working for them. After I hung up the phone, I threw my hands up into the air. Then I called family and friends to tell them I had been offered the job. When I met up with Hamza later, he gave me a hug and said,

"You see that! I told you that you would find a job. I knew you could do it."

Needless to say, things had changed for the better. Finally, here was a chance to change the world and fight for the underdog. I swore to myself that I would do the best job that

I was capable of, and before I'd leave this organization three years later, I would have dedicated most of my waking hours to its work, including working on progress notes and reports at home, progress notes on the train, reading material for work on the train, talking to clients, and taking care of their problems at all hours.

Case visits to families started immediately after my first day. Since Middle Eastern Center was a preventative services agency, the primary purpose of case visits was to make sure that the children I visited were safe and taken care of so that New York State wouldn't have to place them in foster care. In agencies such as Middle Eastern Center, managers will tell you to try to complete all your work between nine and five. Any social worker will tell you that you would be an ill-fit and ineffective employee if you worked just forty hours a week. To be effective, you needed twice the time of a regular work week.

Over the years, my feelings regarding my career choice oscillated. One day I loved the job, and the next, I'd be overwhelmed, but one thing was certain – I worked with unique and unforgettable clients, clients who changed my life. Their victories, defeats, and struggles continue to haunt me. For three years of my life, I had the opportunity to help people from my country of origin, going through the same problems that my family and I had experienced when we came to America.

I also helped abused women to become more independent and hopeful. We worked together to achieve their goals of safety and security for their families. In assisting immigrant women to make sense of their own confusion towards America, I made sense of my own. In working with them, I learned more about myself. I grew as they grew. In fighting for women who wanted to give up, I pulled myself up at the same time. I made them realize that they had left their homeland behind. We were in America now, and in America women couldn't shy away from the world. And yes, they needed to understand that they would be hit here and sometimes hit hard. America, like any other country, was made up of good and bad people. The bad people could take everything from you if you opened yourself up to their darkness – every single part of you, down to your teeth, your skin, and even your soul, could be taken. America was, by no means, free from violence, but I taught them that when you are hit here, you have to fight back because there's so much that you're fighting for – if you can throw off the chains of poverty, then nothing need stand in the way between you what makes you happy, what makes you free. This is what I needed to accept and what I needed to teach my clients.

A few days after my interview, I embarked on my first case visit on a cold and sunny February afternoon with wind whipping against my face. Whether working or unwinding, I found that there was always something wondrous about New York City winters. On that day, Brooklyn students, vendors, and business people headed to their work while others congregated on the street. I walked towards the Court Street subway station. Huge buildings surrounded me, partially blocking out the sunshine. As I walked, bright beams periodically shone through. Having earlier researched where my first visit was, I entered the subway for the proper train. Just like any other time of day, a whole crowd of commuters walked into the subway at the same time as me.

One of the best things about the city was seeing the variety in people wherever you went. The differences in clothing styles, color choices, and fashion in outfits, all the way from Brooklyn to the Bronx, were as wide and diverse as the animal kingdom, and I loved observing all these differences. For me, being able to see this many people, on any given day, satiated a natural curiosity, but I probably wasn't alone in liking the city for this reason. Maybe this is one of the reasons that New York City still calls out to people from all walks of life and from all over the world.

Sitting down in the train, I continued to watch the non-stop activity going on around me. A young man and woman sat across from me and worked together on their laptops. A family, a grandmother, mother, and a baby, sat on the left side of me. The adults spoke to the baby in Chinese. A group of teenagers took up room to my right. Like many other adolescents their age, they talked as if they needed to yell to be heard. A boy started to tease another, and they all laughed.

After I arrived at my stop, I searched for the address where my first home visit would be. Over the years, this first family that I visited, the Hafeez family, would end up being one of the favorite families I worked with. They lived near one of the subway stops of the Q train. I'd hop out of the train with my messenger bag over my shoulder and make my way onto ground level. I'd see so many things when I came to the street, including the stores, the people, and just the general hustle and bustle of the neighborhood. All lined up one next to the other, the stores had colorful signs, lit all day, informing potential customers of what could be found inside. Stores extended their merchandise right onto the street

After exiting the subway, I'd sometimes delay going to the Hafeez's home because I wanted to take in the activity around me. I'd stop in at a food or coffee shop instead of heading straight to my case visit. I enjoyed sitting in Dunkin Donuts or similar store to drink a cup of tea or coffee and take time to reflect on the day. One of the great things about that job was that it allowed me to have a food or caffeine break whenever I wanted – these breaks were necessary because they helped me to recharge for the tremendous amount of work that needed to be accomplished before day's end.

The walk to the Hafeez household, after any breaks, was enjoyable. As I strolled away from the main street, the small yards of houses and apartment complexes started to take up more space. These small green landscapes created an interesting contrast with the rest of the sparse surroundings. Showing up to the Hafeez's, five-story apartment building, I reached for the silver buzzer and rang it, so that someone could let me into the building. This building was similar to many others in Brooklyn, nondescript with a brick façade on the outside. The inside had a large entryway with an ornately styled staircase, with the lowest rung made in the shape of a Doric column. The interior walls were made of brick, stone, and steel. Like other buildings I visited, this one was run down with cracked windows and walls with chipped paint, though the underlying structures remained stable and solid.

To arrive at the Hafeez household, I'd run up four flights of steps and turn right at the end of the stairs. After I rang the bell, I'd typically hear movements inside. Sometimes I'd hear the excited sounds of a baby on the other side. When the door opened, there'd always be a toddler with chubby cheeks standing in the doorway, looking up excitedly to see who it was.

"Step back baby," her mother would say.

The child would typically be wearing traditional South Asian clothing combined with American attire. On my first visit, she wore a pink, American-style shirt, which was one size too tight for her. The front of the shirt read "princess." Below the shirt, she wore a *shalwar*. To top it off, she also wore a pink tutu and princess tiara. She looked up at me with searching and curious eyes. As her mother let me in, the baby walked towards the living room, smiling as she went into the other room. I followed Mrs. Hafeez, a petite woman wearing traditional South Asian clothing, into the living room.

Four other girls sat on the floor. Apparently the family didn't have any furniture. A lot of families I visited in those years lived the same way – they didn't have basic things like furniture or food or clothing.

The girls, sitting in front of me, ranged in age from seven to fourteen. I introduced myself and spoke to them at length.

"Hi everyone. I'm your new Case Planner, Ayesha."

"Are you here to help our family?" one of the older girls asked.

"Yes, I definitely am. I know that things have been difficult lately. I'm sorry you kids have been going through everything you have." I said.

The girls started leaning in to listen more intently. In this job, I found that it didn't take much for kids to listen to you.

"Well, our dad wanted boys. I think that's why he's mad all the time," one of the girls said.

"Well, it doesn't matter what he wanted. He may have wanted boys, but was blessed with seven wonderful girls, right?" I asked them.

They all smiled at me.

"You think so?" one of the younger girls asked.

"Yes, I know so," I said.

"Look at how smart and precious you all are. I bet you all have friends at school and have good grades," I said.

"Our grades are okay, I guess. Jameela's grades could be better though," one of the older girls answered.

"Which one of you is Jameela again?" I asked.

"It's me." The eldest child said.

"Jameela, we will have to work on the grades situation. You know school is very important," I said.

"Yes I know. This year has been really bad. Our father moved out and took all the furniture with him. He's mad at my mom," Jameela said.

"Can you tell me what's been going on?" I asked Mrs. Hafeez.

"He complains about everything and hates me. He took all the furniture. I don't want to live with him anymore. He married me when he was forty, and I was just fifteen. I wish I had gone to school instead of marrying him. Now I need a job, but I don't think anyone will give me a job. I don't know what I'm going to do," she said.

"I will help you find a job," I said.

"But I haven't gone to school," she said.

"I will help you to find a place where you can train for jobs, then. I'm sure that there are job training centers close to you," I said.

"Are you sure they'll take me?" The way she asked the question made it clear that she lacked confidence in herself. Over the course of the year that I worked with her, she would show me other aspects of a damaged self-esteem.

"Let's all work together and make everything in the house awesome," I said to the girls before I left.

The girls all smiled again, and the baby hopped up, came over, and hugged me. I picked up the baby and repeated, "We will make everything awesome, won't we?" The baby shook her head in agreement.

In a week, I went back to the Hafeez household. The girls were all there again and Mrs. Hafeez also sat with us.

"So, how has everything been going, girls?"

The second eldest child, Farah answered and said, "This boy was trying to bully Jameela today, and I told him off. He was making fun of Indians. Why do people think they can just make fun of you? It makes me mad."

"I understand that. I've gone through the same thing. You know what it is, Farah? They are distracted. They aren't focused like we are, right? Try to stay away from bullies, as much as possible, and if they won't leave you alone, then report them to someone in authority like a teacher," I explained.

"Yeah, it's just hard sometimes," Farah said.

"You girls are all wonderful. I don't want you to take anything bad to heart. It has nothing to do with you. If someone is being mean to you, it's their problem, not yours," I said.

Unlike their parents, I had experienced exactly what they were going through. I had grown up in America and knew what the challenges were.

Seeing this as a good opportunity to involve the girls in something positive, I had them take part in a role play. The girls took turns taking on the role of the bully and the person being bullied, and we all thought of different ways that the girls could deal with bullying. The girls liked taking part.

I asked the girls to crowd around a large dry erase board in the living room. I told them that we needed to talk about the importance of education.

"See this girls? I'm drawing a road. This is the journey that we all have to take. There will be many bad things and difficult things that will pop up along the journey, but I'm going to show you how to make it to your destination. Our destination is going to be education."

I proceeded to draw a road and listed issues that the girls could face, such as bullying, crime, parents fighting, not being a boy, no furniture, and lack of money.

"Okay, so we are all going to drive on this road. When you drive on this road, I want you to say what you are doing. This is a very, very important lesson I want all of you to learn. I'm going to go first and show you how to do it. I'm starting on the road now. Someone is trying to bully me, but I have to ignore them because I have to make it to destination education. Look at this girls. Someone just told me that they don't like me, so what should I do?"

"Keep going to destination education." Farah said.

"Very, very good. That's exactly what should be done."

In turn, all the girls had to drive their imaginary car through the windy road to arrive at destination education. Within months, Farah started achieving the best math scores in her grade. The other girl's grades also improved. I told them how wonderful they all were and hoped that the positive reinforcement would stay with them always.

I helped Mrs. Hafeez to build up her self-esteem and stop looking at her abusive marriage as a viable option. Mrs. Hafeez took part in a free employee training program and started working. The last I heard, Mrs Hafeez moved into a new apartment with her daughters and had been living independently from her husband. This family was only one of the many I had an opportunity to serve while I worked at Middle Eastern Center.

Chapter 14
Resurrection

✸ ✸ ✸ ✸ ✸

My time at Middle Eastern Center proved to be a time of learning and during my final year there, an opportunity to go to Europe materialized. My coworker Stacy, a world traveler, had planned a journey to Rome. After speaking with her at length, we decided that I'd join her on her trip. I would have preferred to go with Hamza, but he didn't want to travel outside the United States and wouldn't tell me if he'd ever want to. Italy was always on the top of the list of countries I wanted to visit, so I didn't miss the opportunity to go with Stacy.

Stacy and I weren't close friends, but we both shared an interest in discovery and exploration. The fact that Stacy was so well-travelled made planning the trip easy – she knew how to make a trip to Europe efficient and affordable. Somehow, she managed to find us round trip tickets to Rome for three hundred dollars a person.

Stacy and I left for Rome from Newark International Airport at nine on a Thursday night in April. We stood shoulder to shoulder as we waited for the plane. Fashionably dressed, she took her sunglasses off her head and placed them in her purse. She ran her fingers through her short brown hair.

I boarded the plane behind her, elated at the fact that there was no turning back from this trip. Where once I couldn't so much as drive a mile from my home, I was now flying over the Atlantic Ocean. English started to fade as the primary language, and I heard a flutter of foreign languages ranging from French, Spanish, and Italian. Knowing French, I eavesdropped to see if I could understand what was being said.

Tired from the work week, I fell asleep shortly after takeoff and didn't wake up till we reached Rome. From the moment I stepped off the plane, I was enthralled. I stared out of the airport windows in amazement at the people who went about their day. Men and women walked around speaking Italian. People communicated with each other differently and people dressed differently – fashionable leather shoes, bags, scarves, sunglasses, and belts seemed to be required apparel. Italians were less afraid to experiment with what colors they wore.

Stacy figured out which train we were supposed to catch. She'd already plotted out the route we'd take to our hostel. Looking for guideposts she'd already committed to memory, she assured me she knew exactly where we were going. We took a train from the airport to the central train station in Rome called *Termini*. Stacy directed us to our train, and when we found the right one, we took our seats.

For the entire length of the train ride, all I could see outside the windows was a bright, green, Italian Spring. I took in the tall trees, the lush, open fields and the clear blue sky while continuing to listen to the various languages being spoken around me.

When we arrived at *Termini*, the station was packed with other travelers and commuters. Noticing the structures and edifices surrounding *Termini*, I realized that even the plainest building, in that area, had artistry to it. Still somewhat sleepy from not getting a full night's rest, I felt like I was walking in a beautiful dream.

Stacy had arranged for us to stay at a hostel near the train station. I was uncomfortable with the idea of staying there because hostels had common sleeping and bathroom areas. She assured me that it was a safe and inexpensive way to travel, so I tried to stop worrying about it.

We looked at her map together and started heading in the direction of the hostel. It's this way," Stacy said. As we walked, I looked around taking in the surrounding architecture. On top of one of the buildings was a massive, golden figure of Christ. The figure had a halo, over its head, and an outstretched hand. I pointed the statue out to Stacy.

During the course of my week in the "eternal city," the statue often helped me find where I was going. When I was lost, I'd look up and experience great relief when I saw the statue with its hand calmly outstretched. It helped me out of moments of panic, and when I saw the statue, I'd think to myself "thank goodness." By the end of my trip, I began to suspect that the statue had been erected, in part, to encourage conversion to Christianity. It was Rome after all.

After walking a few minutes, we turned right onto the street where our hostel was. Arriving at the front door, we saw what looked like an official notice. Even though neither of us could speak Italian, it became clear that the notice was from the police. For once, Stacy seemed at a loss.

"I don't know what's going on. The door is locked, so we can't go in to find out. Let's figure out what's happening," she said.

Standing near the hostel was a group of middle-aged men dressed in traditionally South Asian clothing. I went over and asked if they spoke Urdu. One of the men started to speak to me in Urdu.

"We're supposed to stay in this building and no one is answering our knocks," I said.

"The police came in the morning and closed it," the man answered.

"Do you know what happened and why the police came?" I asked.

"No, I'm not sure, but there was a bunch of police here, and they closed the building," he said. I thanked the group and came back to Stacy.

"How useful it can be to know another language," I thought to myself. There I was, in a foreign country where most people spoke Italian, yet my ability to speak Urdu was what was helping us out of a stressful situation.

I went back over to Stacy who still stood at the front door of the hostel.

"It's definitely closed," I told her.

"Did they say why?"

"They don't know what happened. We're going to have to find a place to stay. Do you think we'll have a problem?"

"I don't know, but we should be fine. We should be able to find another place to stay," she said.

We walked away from the hostel, deciding we needed to arrange a hotel room. We walked towards the center of town again. The streets weren't like any I had ever seen before – the streets in Rome seemed more like museums than streets.

"Look at that, Stacy," I said pointing to a building.

We saw a Best Western and were quickly able to book a room. From that point on, Stacy and I explored Rome on our own. During the day, I'd walk the entire length of the city by myself. I observed and drew meaning from everything around me. I saw people, art, and architecture of unforgettable beauty. I stood in outdoor cafes drinking delicious beverages and tasting new foods. In the midst of this achievement, this ability to explore a foreign city by myself, I realized that I didn't need anyone to lean on, that I could stand on my own. Later on, it became clear that my trip to Rome was a gift – I was meant to discover my own independence and that I had become capable and strong.

Following the pattern of my life like clockwork, my glorious time in Rome was followed by disappointment after I returned to the United States. The state of my marriage had been slowly deteriorating, though the first year with my husband had been fun and involved good conversation, watching movies, dining out, and traveling within the United States. Serious problems started cropping up after two years.

Hamza proved to be a critical spouse, and nothing I did was exactly as he wanted, so he lectured me about how I could improve myself. At first his advice was endearing, but later, it became tiring. I found out that marriage wasn't magical and that I was the same woman I'd always been. Fear started to set in, and I wondered if my marriage would succeed in a life where failure felt like the norm. Instead of making me more positive, like I thought it would, marriage made me more negative. An unprecedented combination of anger and sadness started to overcome me since I lost the hope that marriage would change my life and make me into someone new.

Before we married, Hamza asked me if I'd enjoy socializing with his friends. I told him that I looked forward to meeting his friends but was inwardly apprehensive about doing so. Would I have *anything* in common with his friends, especially his male friends? My whole life, up until that point, had revolved around female friends because having boys or men around was unacceptable according to my parents. I hoped that marriage would change Hamza and that after we married, he wouldn't care if I socialized or not, but he did care and disapproved of my introversion.

One day, I yelled out "Please don't divorce me!"

"*What* are you *talking* about?" he asked.

"Are you going to divorce me?" I asked.

"I can't believe you're asking that question. What is wrong with you? Why would you ask this kind of question?" he asked.

"I don't know. You keep pointing out all these things that you don't like about me," I said.

"I'm going to go for a walk," he said and left.

After three years, I was filled with unexpected cynicism. My marriage became a familiar battleground, and the same war began again. Hamza and I fought and belittled each other, but wasn't it supposed to be us against the world? He should have been home with me, criticizing societal problems and trying to find ways to contribute and make things better. Why weren't we more like my parents who always wanted social justice for everyone? What about changing the world? I realized, though, that he didn't need to worry about changing the world. Unlike me, he had grown up in a relatively privileged background in Karachi. There, he had always fit in, so now his confidence was unwavering.

And my interest in learning did nothing but anger him. One evening after work, I went to Strand Book Store and ended up with a couple of great finds. Afterwards, I met Hamza at a nearby Italian restaurant. Pulling out one of the books I'd bought, the *Canterbury Tales*, I showed him the detailed artwork, on both the cover and inside pages.

"You know this book is essential in regards to the development of the English language," I said. For a few seconds, Hamza remained quiet.

Then he asked, "What is wrong with you?"

"What's your problem?" I responded.

"I'm here in a great restaurant, in one of the most fabulous cities in the world, and you're trying to discuss a goddamned book! This isn't the place to talk about a stupid book. You just use education as an escape from life," he said.

"I should be able to talk about this here if I want, but fine! I'll put the book away!" I was silent for the rest of our time at the restaurant. If he didn't understand my love of learning, then he clearly didn't understand me. Learning could give hope when there was none.

Also, the way I dressed, modest and practical, bothered Hamza. Like everyone else in the world, he also had strong opinions on how women, particularly his wife, should dress. My parents appreciated my modesty in dress, but Hamza wanted me to put on makeup, wear high heels, and tighter clothing. His ideal woman, like many other Pakistani men of his generation who had grown up watching James Bond movies, was that of a tall, thin, sexy blond woman in a fancy ball gown and high heels. To these men, Bond girls were powerful and alluring, and this was what Hamza wanted me to become, but how or why would I want to be something so different than myself? How could I wear what those girls wore? Glitz and glam had their place, but I found no overwhelming reason or cause that would propel me to put on a pair of stilettos. And just like so many other men of his generation, Hamza gave into his mother and married the type of woman she wanted him to, not the kind of woman he actually wanted. I wondered how many other South Asian women, taught to be modest by their parents, ended up with men who couldn't stand their modesty in dress and personality. How many of them actually ended up with nobody, not even their husband, understanding them.

"What you're wearing makes you look ridiculous. It's like you're wearing clown pants. You would look better if you wore something more fitting. Also, try wearing small heels, at least," Hamza said.

"I don't want to, and heels make me uncomfortable. I have flat feet. My outfit is fine," I said.

"No, it's not," he said, grinding his teeth.

In one conversation, Hamza brought up how beautiful he thought Scarlet Johannsen was. In another, he went on and on about Liv Tyler or Emily Blunt. I agreed with him. Undeniably, these women were visions of beauty, but clearly, I wouldn't look like them no matter what I did. I was pretty, but I would never be a white woman, the standard of beauty for many and most importantly, the standard of beauty for my husband.

"You're never going to be happy with me. I can't look the way you so desperately need your wife to look, for some reason. You put so much pressure on me. What you really always wanted was something I cannot be. There is no way for me to look like what you want, Scarlett Johannsen or Liv Tyler or Emily Blunt. You are drawn to the aesthetic of white women, and I will never be a white woman," I said, angry that he wasn't even self-aware enough to know his own preferences.

After the constant back and forth on changing the way I dressed, I become irritated, and a surprisingly conservative streak kept emerging in me. So, the more time that went by, the more time he spent with his friends at bars, especially at his favorite hangout, *Bar and Books*. I never went on these outings with him because after going with him to *Bar and Books*, for the first time, I learned that I hated the smell of hard liquor and cigars, or sitting, for hours on end, in dark, loud places and not doing anything productive.

"I don't want to be like the women at *Bar and Books*, okay. Stop asking me to hang out with your boyfriends. My parents never wanted me to spend that much time with men, and now you want me sit on their laps, at a freaking cigar bar. Stop trying to make me go there. It's not a place for ladies," I said.

I wanted to change him and to make him more centered like me. I walked the line between the traditional Pakistani world and the American one. I found a good balance that wasn't too far to one side or the other. Why couldn't he do the same thing?

"What the hell are you talking about? There's nothing wrong with you hanging out with my friends or going out to Bar and Books. You're crazy," he said.

The irony was that his family, who thought he was the perfect Pakistani son, didn't know anything about how he lived, including the fact that he couldn't go one night without drinking hard liquor. I was looking at the endgame and wanted him to live a long life with me. I would have taken care of him, if he did become sick, but tried to warn him about his drinking habits before it took a toll on his health.

"Drinking that shit every night isn't good for you. You're going to get cirrhosis by the time you're fifty. By the way, how come your sister doesn't have to do any of that stuff with men? How come your sister can sit at home, nice and safe in her house? How come she can read and write in her spare time without being given dirty looks. And what about your mother for that fact. She is a professor for God's sake. How come they don't have to sit on men's laps?" I continued.

"Don't bring my family into this?" he warned.

"Why, is your sister exempt? If you don't want to think about her in heels or at parties, being forced to talk to random men, then stop trying to force me into it. Maybe I want to live like your sister does. Or maybe she doesn't live like that. Maybe your mother doesn't either. Maybe your mom goes to *Bar and Books* to sit on men's laps," I said.

"I'm warning you! Stop right now," he said.

I realized that he meant that he would hit me if I continued, but I had a point to prove, so I kept going. There was a loud "whaaaaap" as his hand slammed into my face. My head moved downwards, and, in front of me, I saw a hundred glimmering, white lights. Immersed into an immediate silence, I started falling into that beautiful light, finally leaving everything behind. After a few moments, my vision returned to normal, and I felt the pain in my face. As I regained my balance, I looked up.

"I told you to stop," he said and walked away.

Though I could have called the police in retaliation, I didn't. A wife wasn't supposed to ruin her husband's life by calling the police, but if I had to do it over again, I would have called the police and left him. Or, I would have hit him back, like he deserved. I'd have given him a good fight. I'd have done anything other than allowing him to walk away.

At the time, I didn't realize how depressed I truly was. I couldn't face the fact that a real husband wouldn't treat his wife this way. A real husband would never hit, no matter the circumstance. Yet, I kept trying to save the marriage because I thought that things could improve and become the way they were during our first year together. "It was the drinking that had changed him. If only I could help him stop drinking," I thought to myself.

After observing my state one afternoon, my parents spoke to me out of concern.

"You don't seem well. What is wrong with you?" my mother asked, staring at me from across a table at an Indian restaurant in Jersey City. Families walked in, heading to the buffet at the front of the restaurant, and pointed to specific, steel bins to indicate to the employees which food items they wanted. The walls were covered in a light green paint and colorful streamers, hung from the ceilings and walls.

"Nothing's wrong except that my life never turns out well. I'm meant to suffer. I just have to come to terms with that. I should stop expecting anything and just give up," I said weeping into a napkin.

"Habib – What is wrong with her? Look at her. She's so pale," my mother said.

"She's sad. He isn't taking care of her, like I thought he would," my father said.

"*Beta*, you need to see a counselor. I'm worried about you," my mother said.

As a result of this conversation, I spoke to a psychiatrist who diagnosed me with anxiety and depression. I started taking antidepressants, which changed my outlook, and although I was still stoic, my negative emotions became tempered. I refocused on hobbies and goals. In terms of my marriage, I become less combative and tried to change the things that Hamza disliked about me, but, according to him, I still couldn't do anything right.

After three years of marriage though, I started to wonder if Hamza had only married me so he could attain permanent residency in the United States. His attitude changed drastically for the worst after I signed paperwork for his permanent residency status, which my parents told me not to do. I couldn't imagine anyone being so sinister, yet he avoided any effort to improve the marriage after his paperwork went through. I tried to spend time with him, but he refused to do anything with me. I suggested marriage counseling, but he rejected the idea every time.

Three years into the marriage, Hamza asked "Don't you want something more out of life?"

"What do you mean?" I asked.

"Well, you have been working at the same job, for almost the same pay, for two years," he said.

"Oh – that's what you're talking about. Yes, I'm perfectly happy working where I work. I *help* people! I make an impact and change people's lives. I might work there forever. Money isn't everything, you know," I said sarcastically.

Receiving a social worker's salary didn't bother me. I wanted a simple life, living in a small comfortable home, maybe in New Jersey, where I could spend my free time watching movies, reading books, or learning more about a particular language. I didn't need glitz and glam. I didn't need a large supply of money to fund an endless party.

By this point, my parents lectured me in surprisingly progressive way. My dad said things like,

"He doesn't speak about a future with you, he doesn't want to share information about his bank accounts with you, he doesn't want to have children with you, and he doesn't want to buy a house with you. There is something wrong here. I think you have a con man on your hands. If you want to stop the paperwork for his visa, do it now. Go tell the government the truth. Tell them how he doesn't come home at night and how he acts like he's single. If you want to divorce him, we will completely understand."

In discussing my marriage with my parents, I had actually become the conservative one, and even though they told me that it was okay to end the marriage, I didn't agree.

"I know everything is rocky right now, but I don't think that he is doing all this to con me. This is just how he is. I want to work on the marriage, and maybe, things will improve. Maybe things will be like they were that first year," I told my parents.

During my trip to Rome, Hamza hired a divorce attorney and told me about it when I returned home. Just like the self-esteem of anyone who isn't able to make their marriage work, my self-esteem took a blow. I kept trying to improve the marriage, and in this vain attempt to fix things, dispensed so much needless effort. Unlike me, Hamza realized that our relationship had ended long before we divorced. Yet, I continued to suffer. Years after he was done with me, he still wouldn't tell the truth, baiting me into fight after fight, until even just being acquaintances was no longer possible.

In the last few weeks of us living together, Hamza said, "I know that you've been trying to make a lot of changes, but it just isn't enough. Divorce is better for both of us. This is what has to happen."

"Now that you have your Green Card, it has to happen, right?" I asked.

He had these conversations with me in a succinct manner, almost as if something or someone was waiting for him. It was as if he wanted to finish with the formality of being married to me and return to his real life, and although I suspected it, I could never prove infidelity.

"No one in my family has ever been divorced before," I said.

"The only reason I stayed in this marriage so long is because I felt a responsibility towards you. I felt like you were so sensitive that the world would crush you, and you wouldn't be able to take care of yourself if I left, but better now than later," he said.

"Why can't you just go to marriage counseling with me? Why won't you even try?" I asked.

Pursing his lips, he said, "It just won't work. I am moving out soon, so you should find a new place too," he said as he walked out of the apartment.

Infidelity, cruelty, and violence are justified reasons for a divorce, but I hadn't been guilty of any of these, so why was I being divorced? I didn't believe in divorce, and marriage was a place where an unexpectedly conservative side of me emerged. I believed in the commitment that marriage represented, and I would never have considered abandoning a spouse under any circumstances, even if he lost his health, his money, or his mind. This is what I would have undoubtedly done because this is what *I had promised*. Hamza didn't deserve my loyalty, but he had it because I believed the promise to marry someone was a sacred trust. I wasn't giving Hamza, the individual, my faith and loyalty. Rather, I was giving the person who I had signed a marriage contract with what they were supposed to have, unquestioningly.

Even though divorce was an extremely difficult process, I didn't blame the beautiful and flirtatious women who could be found in any bar in New York City, and I don't blame the woman who started dating Hamza shortly after, and perhaps even before, our divorce. I do, however, blame my ex-husband for always knowing, in his heart, that he wanted a certain type of woman, which I was not, and marrying me anyway. Perhaps none of these things mattered because, maybe, he just needed to marry someone to attain residency in the United States, and he chose me to be the woman to use for this end.

I also wished my father hadn't created a picture of husbands, in my mind, which was unrealistic. I superimposed all of the good traits of husbands, which my father described, onto a selfish man who had no loyalty, a man who didn't come anywhere close to my father's ideal.

When the day of the divorce finally came, I felt deep regret. Hamza, on the other hand, sat comfortably and made small talk with his lawyer. Saddened by the idea that my marriage would end that day, I sobbed into my hands. Watching me, my mother couldn't help crying as well. I could tell that my father felt equally bad, but he expressed his emotions in a different way. When my mother and I cried, he said, "Why are you both so upset? This is a good thing. Hamza was a con-artist, Ayesha, and I'm sorry I didn't realize it earlier," he said.

"I'm sad because my marriage failed. Why are you so sure he is a con-artist?" I asked.

"After everything he's done, how can you think he is anything but?" my father asked.

"Everything was good in the beginning though. He seemed happy, and we were happy, and then, all of a sudden, something changed," I sobbed.

"Use your logic. You're still thinking emotionally. If you use logic, you'll see the situation for what it is," my father said.

Earlier that day, Hamza found out what my father thought of him. For my father, there was no grey area here, just black and white. In his mind, what Hamza had done was wrong. While Hamza wore a blue tailor-made suit, a checkered shirt with blue and brown lines, a pin-dot tie, and leather shoes, my dad walked in wearing a Philadelphia Eagle's cap, black sneakers, and casual clothing. Hamza and my father had shared a mutual respect in previous years, and although Hamza was still ready to be respectful, my dad didn't feel the same way. As we walked past Hamza, he tried to greet my parents, as he always did, to which my father responded with a prolonged scowl, followed by utter silence. In that moment, I realized that my dad may have been more disillusioned by the end of my marriage than I was. It made sense. Although he had always lectured me about being cautious with people, he never followed his own advice because thinking the best of other people came naturally to him. He had always trusted Hamza until he saw that he couldn't.

Although they were dressed up, Hamza and his lawyer treated the divorce very casually, talking, telling jokes to each other, and laughing. His lawyer helped to break up marriages all the time, like she did with mine, but she didn't think anything of it. I was sad about having a failed marriage, but not so sad that I couldn't loathe their nonchalance.

Regardless of all the regrets, I really didn't have anything to be sorry about. I fought to save a marriage in which the other party put in little to no effort, and regardless of his unpleasant, abusive, and overly-critical ways, I hadn't given up on the marriage because I wasn't a quitter. And although I'll never know the truth, maybe there really was a reason that it was impossible to save my marriage.

A few months after my divorce, I'd see something that could have been the cause of my breakup. Going through my old Facebook messages, I came across my ex-husband's profile page, but he wasn't standing alone. Standing with him was my replacement, and she was everything that I wasn't. Her blue eyes flashed with unwavering confidence, and her brown hair was well styled. She seemed posh and fashionable. Curious about her career, I searched the internet and found out that she was a journalist in the magazine-publishing world. In the picture, my ex-husband looked at her with a look of pride that was never directed at me. So much can be gathered from one picture, and a photo can be as piercing as the most pointed words. The picture spoke to me and said:

I was right, and you were wrong. You were holding me back. Here's a woman that measures up. She's everything that you could never be. I prefer her over any version of you because you are nothing, and she is everything. We're going to be married and live happily while you will fade alone and unloved. I hope you disappear fully into the darkness that's always called out to you.

The traditional part of me couldn't help but feel that I'd been ruined. With my divorce, I hadn't just lost my present but also my past. All the years of sacrifice, loneliness, and restriction now seemed useless. It had turned out that I'd been waiting for *nothing, nothing at all. In life, there never was and never would be any certainty from the world of people.* My family and friends told me that the divorce was a good thing, but no one fully comprehended the gravity of what had taken place. Unlike most of my peers, I'd grown up with the hope that I was "holding out" for something wonderful while my American counterparts experienced everything that life had to offer – my peers lived their lives to the fullest, taking whatever benefits and consequences came their way. On the other hand, immigrant children, like me, lived in a constant state of guilt because the surrounding fulfillment was supposed to be a distraction to be ignored. Yet, if I had to do it over again and had always been in charge of my own life, I would still have followed a lot of my parent's rules, but broken some as well. I would have allowed my younger self to travel to different cities and countries with friends and classmates, drive before I was twenty-one, and play on sport's teams to my heart's content.

If I was still in Pakistan, something like a divorce could really have ruined me. It would certainly have affected how people, especially conservative people, viewed me, but, luckily, this was America, and most people didn't blink an eye when they found out that I was divorced. For most, I still had my dignity as a human being.

Six months after the divorce, any money I'd saved up quickly dissolved. Although my financial position had improved with marriage, I'd never felt completely secure. After my divorce though, my anxiety about money came back. My parents had helped me to pay for my expensive lawyer's fees, but my other bills, which were manageable when I was married, were now impossible to keep up with.

Luckily, during the divorce proceedings, I secured a few years of alimony although Hamza actually starting the payments was like pulling teeth. Payments were skipped, so that bills went unpaid and credit cards were closed. I quit my job because rent for my apartment, along with my other bills, made it difficult for me to even make it to work. The expense of commuting back and forth from New Jersey to Brooklyn, which included bus and subway fares, or tolls if I drove, was too high.

After a year of struggling to be on time with bills, alimony became regular, and I started receiving sixteen-hundred dollars a month. I decided not to go back to work. Alimony allowed me to slow down and take a break. So, I was back to where I began, but this fact was as liberating as it was devastating. I was finally *free* because I no longer had to deal with my ex-husband's constant pressure to become something that I was not. It was as if I had finally been set free from some sort of spell. I no longer had any ties or responsibility to the man I'd been married to, a man who was not strong enough to stay with a wife in her elemental form, a woman who could be socially anxious or argumentative or full of self-doubt but also one who wanted to save the world and was full of love and compassion and loyalty. He had really set me free, free to find the one who would be strong enough; I would find that one, or I would stand on my own feet forever because I would never accept less than what is deserved by any good woman or man, support and loyalty from those who they are in relationship with. And if anyone ever raised a hand to me again, even if I pushed their buttons, then that person would deal with an equal and opposite reaction.

I'd done everything that everyone asked of me, up until that point, but now I wanted to determine my own direction. It was finally time for me to start living by my own rules, and that's just what I started to do. When my parents told me that I should move back in with them, since it was the proper thing for a single woman to do, I refused. I didn't want to hurt their feelings, but I needed to live on my own and learn how to deal with the world.

Wanting a more comfortable place to live than my apartment in West New York, New Jersey, with its closeness to the apartment that I'd shared with my ex-husband in the neighboring town of Weehawken, I moved back to Pennsylvania. It wasn't until I secured a tiny apartment in Lansdale, which was located minutes from North Penn High School, that I truly started to recover from the past. My new, cozy, carpeted, ground-floor apartment was affordable, which put my mind at ease, and its small size discouraged loneliness because its hundred and ninety square feet of space was intended for a single person. The sun beamed into the tiny room that was my apartment, coating the furniture and cream-colored carpet with light. If I wanted to go out into the sun, I could open a sliding door onto the apartment complex's central lawn.

I kept the bare essentials – a box spring and mattress, a desk, a computer, a small cabinet, and television. My books were neatly stacked in a sectioned-off area of the apartment. My clothing, shoes, and accessories were easily stored in a walk-in closet. I didn't want much more than this – I needed to reflect and the less material I had around me, the better.

During this year, a year in which I lost so much, I found something that gave me profound relief – writing. Everything that had been bottled up inside of me searched desperately for an outlet. Words suddenly started gushing out of my crippled psyche the way that blood flows out of a deep knife wound. For me, a person in a constant battle with depression, finding an outlet like writing was not just a hobby but a way to survive.

So, *there really was one certainty in life*. Regardless of everything I went through, including being left out or made fun of or being called ugly or crazy, there was something that refused to give up, something that still yearned for a better life and better self, something that grasped at activities like writing to create joy out of sadness and belonging out of exclusion, and something that showed me in dreams and hopes what I could still be. It was something that kept prodding me and pushing me to realize that no matter the turmoil, or even abuse, I could stand on my own feet and survive. It was what prevented me from harming myself as a child.

In 2011, I started attending an MFA program in creative writing at Rosemont College. As time went by, I found out that attending this program was one of the best decisions I'd ever made. A few months after my first class, a certain calm finally descended. The combination of a low-key lifestyle, including living in a simple and comfortable apartment near my family and pursuing a degree in something interesting to me was exactly what I needed.

My first winter break away from the MFA program was when everything seemed to stabilize and settle into place. I could finally see the beginning of a new life. Still not working,

I became fully focused on school. I researched, read, watched movies, and wrote. During that month away from school, I'd wake up extremely early, before anyone else was up, even before the twilight. After washing my face and brushing my teeth, I'd put on my black and red checkered coat, a sweater, pants, and a fleece cap. Exiting my apartment building, I'd take in the fresh air and breathe out, watching the white vapor in front of me. The winter morning, with its cold, brought with it an overwhelming feeling of possibility. Again, I looked forward to another semester, imagining what I would read, write, and learn. What would this program mean for me, and what kind of woman would I be when I finished? What would I discover while I wrote, read, and prepared for classes? Would I meet others who would support the woman I was becoming, a woman who loved others but was also finally learning to love herself too?

After entering my car, I'd turn on the heat which would take a few seconds to warm, and I'd put on music, The Cure or Tori Amos, to distract me. Looking out in front of me, I'd notice the uniform, white brick of the apartment complex. The free-standing lights would still be on, and an Acme supermarket, across from my apartment, added more light to the early morning. I'd start the drive to the local convenience store and, after a few minutes, arrive at Wawa. In the dark, the store's lights would glow in the middle of what seemed like row upon row of unending field, but the building wouldn't stand out. Instead, it seemed perfectly placed, an island of order with everything I needed, in the sparse movements of the morning. Always polite, the workers in Wawa usually smiled and said good morning to me. Their morning salutations contributed to a growing sense of peace. I'd usually buy a cup of coffee and breakfast, which cost me a little under five dollars. Enjoying my breakfast, I'd look out onto the open fields and think about all the possibilities for my future.

Epilogue

Years ago, I came to this country with my family, and at that time, none of us were fully capable of understanding America, so we worked together to grow and overcome our challenges. Sometimes, we faced the world alone, making our own independent journeys towards our dreams. Since then, we've all changed tremendously.

Yes, I arrived here an immigrant, but now, there are parts of me that are nothing else than American. But my other self, that quiet "Indian girl," isn't gone – she continues to dwell in me as I walk the line between my two selves, tipping one way or the other depending on the circumstance. By no means have I figured everything out, but I've learned, grown, and supported others along the way. I hope my small contributions have helped to make the world a better place. My story is not one of phenomenal success. Rather, it is a journey of small steps towards total self-acceptance. I walked on a confusing road, filled with mixed messages, which sometimes drained my enthusiastic nature, but I didn't retreat into the dark and convincing calm that called out to me.

I didn't give up, and though it felt that I'd never belong, I did find belonging and genuine friends to share my life with, people who love me the way I am. Though my marriage failed, I didn't give up on the idea finding understanding, loyalty, and faith from another. And all the learning I had access to, whether it was in college or graduate school, gave me the tools I needed to create meaningfully.

For me, every disappointment and success I've had has helped me to stand on my own, so that I can choose what I want out of life. Though at first fearful of my independence, my parents are now proud of the strong woman I've become. I continue to be inspired by their strength and their ability to adapt to a place so different than where they grew up.

Still, I sometimes wonder what our lives would have been like if my parents had never left Pakistan. Moving to America, at an early age, gave me both great joy and sadness that I probably wouldn't have experienced otherwise. In Pakistan, I'd most likely have lived much more comfortably, as the wife of an engineer or doctor and the mother of a few children, just like my own mother and grandmother before me. At the same time, I wouldn't have had a reason to write this book, which has been an irreplaceable experience. I consider being able to remember, honor, and celebrate my journey my greatest success. I am most thankful to have written something that, in some way, could inspire or help others who stumble through *The Borderland Between Worlds*.

Acknowledgements

First, I would like to thank Richard D. Bank, my highly esteemed professor, for his encouragement and inspiration and also to Krish Singh, Publisher at Auctus, for his valuable guidance and patience during the preparation of this manuscript. Without Krish Singh, whose goal is to publish authors whose works don't fit neatly with commercial publishers, my dream of publishing this work might have been put on the back shelf forever. Thank you, Richard, for helping me learn every aspect of the oftentimes difficult craft of creative nonfiction and for helping me to confront and use difficult memories to create this book. From my first creative nonfiction class at Rosemont College to submitting my thesis, a first-draft of this book, you were a guiding light. Also, thank you for introducing me to Auctus Publishers. Thank you Krish for making the publishing process accessible, efficient, and ethical and for publishing those who continue to be underrepresented in traditional publishing.

I would also like to thank the following people without whom this book would not have been possible: my family, including my beloved parents. Carla Spataro, Director of the MFA program at Rosemont College, without whose kind, caring, and supportive leadership, I wouldn't have gotten to this point in my career. Anne Converse Willkomm and her intelligent guidance during my time at Rosemont's publishing program. I would also like to thank Asma Rizwan and family, Asma Bashir, Ali, Jeremy, Seth, and Adam Santo and Joshua Ginsberg, Alice Shan and the Shan family, Aliya Siddiqui and the Siddiqui family, Anam Shah, Angel Keene, Anne Kaier, Ardis Lukens, Barbara Lonnquist, Carlos José Pérez Sémano, Catt and Shawn Colborn, Carol Lott, Christy Tappert and Alex, Christine Obst, Cristina Utti and the Utti family, Courtney Bambrick, Cecelia Cavanaugh, Elaine Paliatsas-Haughey, Erin Kelly, Eileen Moeller, Emily Gavigan, Gail Cathey, Heather Fix, Holly Caldwell, Janice Merendino, Jacqui Hopkins, Jamisha Simmons, Jodi Brown, Jennifer Candipan, Jen Breen, Kelly Woods, Kim and Ben Grandizio, K.J. Wells, Lana Barash and family, Laura Hough, Lena Alhusseini, Lindsey Davis, Linda

Romanowski, Lena Van, Liz Abrams-Morley, Mary-Jo Larkin, Mary Helen Kashuba, Marilyn Sori, Marian Ehnow, Maria Ceferatti, Molly Lazer, Michael Pfister, Melanie Allen, Nancy Kotkin, Nathene Pogach, Patricia Whittaker, Parveen Fakhruddin and family, Pietra Dunmore, Rabia Khan, Roman Colombo, Robin Goman, Saher Sandhu, Shumi Khan, Sharon Browning, Sara Kitchen, Sister Mary Darah, Spencer Shaak, Suzanne Conway, Tori Bond, Aliya Rogers, Andrea Blau, Julie Deputy, Julie Wade, Lejla Ibrahimpasic, Marilyn Martinez, Isabella Stich, Nikki Bailey, Jen Lott, Nalani Drakes, the Eldridge family including Sarah and Emily, Amanda Mooney, Marie Baptiste, Jordan Blum, M.M. Wittle, Surayya Aftab and family, Cynthia Perkel, Tony Della Pietra, Emily London, Natalie Dizon, Kinaja Janardhanan, Krista Heinrich, Elena Holmes, the Wasson family including Colleen and Katie, Jessica Bergey, Maureen Barnes, Angi Didanato Mustschler, Susan LJ, Francine Albert, Colin Likens, Kathleen Staley, Tisha Clarke, George and Peggie Preston, Timothy Shortell, Valerie Woods, Bret Denning, Paul Eisenhauer, Rita Michael Scully, Laura Paul, Isabella Stich, Tia Noelle Pratt, Fayza Tazeen Charette, Emily Begrich. Though we may not talk every day, I thank you for the profound things you've done to help me in my journey.

CPSIA information can be obtained
at www.ICGtesting.com
Printed in the USA
LVHW020104280120
645025LV00013B/1315